W9-BNA-700

Instructor's Notes

Everything's an Argument
with Readings

Instructor's Notes

Everything's an Argument with Readings

Fourth Edition

Andrea A. Lunsford
John J. Ruszkiewicz
Keith Walters

Prepared by John Kinkade, Jodi Egerton,
and Taryne Hallett

Manufactured in the United States of America.

1 0 9 8 7
f e d c b a

For information write: Bedford/St. Martin's, 75 Arlington Street, Boston, MA 02116   (617-399-4000)

ISBN-10: 0-312-45169-5
ISBN-13: 978-0-312-45169-1

Contents

Making a Visual Argument: Three Views on Body Image

Chapter 22: How Does the Media Stereotype *You*?   79
Making a Visual Argument: Artists and Comics
Take On Stereotyping

Chapter 25: What Does Your Language Say about Your Identity? 139

Making a Visual Argument: Public Service Campaigns Use Language to Send a Message

Introduction

The title of this text—*Everything's an Argument*—is more than just a snappy phrase. It represents our conviction that all language, whether written or spoken, visual or textual, is *motivated*. Because language is a human activity and because humans exist in a complex world of goals, purposes, and activities, language cannot be anything *but* motivated. In the words of Kenneth Burke, whose work has been central to the conception of this text, language is a form of "symbolic action": it gets things done in the world, acting on people and situations. The weak version of this argument claims simply that language has effects in the world or that people use language to accomplish ends; most of us would have no difficulty accepting that proposition.

But we hold to the strong version of the argument, maintaining, with Burke, that all language is *inherently* a form of argument. In this formulation of the claim, people use language to create *identification* between themselves and their audience. We cannot escape this naturally human function of language. The flip side of the argument that all language is motivated is powerful, too: all language is open to interpretation and negotiation. Production and analysis of language in this model require not just reason but also all the sensory faculties and an awareness of the rhetor's and the audience's history and experiences. Burke's definition of language's scope and power makes apparently simple activities—chatting with friends, reading the newspaper, writing a note to yourself—into scenes of argument and identification. We are all "wordlings," made of language as much as users of it.

In *A Grammar of Motives*, Burke introduced the dramatistic pentad, a way of describing the human uses of language and the relationships among people, their language, and their world. The five elements—act, scene, agent, agency, purpose—do not appear explicitly in this text, but the concepts remain important to us. The text's focus on the ethical problems of language use reflects our sense that responsible argument always considers the rhetorical situation in all its fullness; without attention to the ethical positions writers and readers inhabit, rhetoric—productive *and* analytic—is irresponsible. We hope that this text will help students learn to use language well, as readers and as writers, and that students will come to understand the complex role language plays in their life and world.

The Structure of the *Instructor's Notes*

The text of these notes is arranged to follow the text chapter by chapter. Each chapter's notes outline some of the problems you might face while teaching the chapter, suggest some solutions, and address the chapter exercises, with ideas for extending those exercises beyond the text. The exercises are open-ended, so our notes are, too: there are no easy answers to any of the problems we suggest in each chapter. (Please note that a few exercises, those which might elicit especially varied responses, are not addressed in these notes.)

At the close of each chapter are cross references to i•claim: Visualizing Argument or for i•cite: Visualizing Sources multimedia CD-ROMs, with suggestions for specific assignments that support each chapter. Both i•cite and i•claim are available for free when packaged with the book (see the back cover of these Notes for packaging information).

Notes for Using the Readings

You've already noticed that the collection of readings in *Everything's an Argument with Readings* is quite different from the collections of readings in other rhetoric texts. Consistent with the title of the book, the *EAR* readings include traditional essays as well as arguments in other genres—newspaper articles, poems, cartoons, Web sites, and more. Some genres may be unfamiliar at first, but we hope you will discover, as we have, that the variety gives you a great deal of flexibility and allows you to approach argumentation from fresh perspectives that can help your students readily grasp the value of rhetoric in real-life applications.

Each chapter's readings contains at least one traditional essay that can serve as a model of the kind of writing that students are learning to produce. News pieces can be especially valuable for helping students learn to identify authors' points of view, even in contexts where the writer's stance isn't overtly stated. In the Response questions following each reading students may be asked to find and state the positions taken in the journalistic pieces, or they may be asked to redraft an argument into academic essay format. Such exercises have a threefold purpose — to test comprehension, to assist students in understanding the importance of style and tone in various genres, and to give students practice in crafting academic prose. An additional value of these exercises is that they incorporate ideas and conclusions already provided by the reading, thereby enabling students to focus strictly on the craft of writing.

The chapter topics were chosen for their currency in public discourse and for their complexity. None of them can be considered a simple pro/con question or a clear-cut issue of conventional conservative/liberal opposition. We expect one of the benefits of this variety to be that the alliances among students in your classroom discussions throughout the term will shift with the various topics, allowing students to both acquaint themselves with a broader range of ideas and find commonality with a broader range of people than they might otherwise. The readings within each chapter contribute to that complexity both by their content and by the variety of genres and media represented.

The questions following the readings are quite varied, although there is at least one writing assignment for nearly every reading. Many questions require students to synthesize information from other readings in the same chapter. Most of the questions, except where stated otherwise, are intended for individual responses. In addition, many of them can provide focus for classroom discussion or small group work.

Using the *Instructor's Notes*

Each of the eight chapters of readings has a corresponding chapter in the *Notes* that provides suggested answers to the questions following each reading. Each chapter of the *Notes* begins with an introduction to the issues addressed in the chapter, along with some general questions that the issues raise. At the end of each chapter are wrap-up exercises that incorporate material from two or more readings; some of these questions would be suitable for in-class essay writing. We also provide a suggested classroom exercise for each reading.

Key to Questions, Answers, and Exercises

For every chapter, we provide possible answers to the questions at the end of each reading and also suggest a classroom exercise for each reading. Most questions are quite open-ended, and the answers will vary; in many cases we've suggested one or more possibilities. No attempt has been made to provide answers for writing assignments.

The concept behind the classroom exercises is to give each reading a session's worth (about an hour) of class time, although you may be budgeting class time very differently. Except where otherwise noted, the exercises are discussion questions based on the reading. Some of the classroom exercises focus on the content of the reading, some require students to think about the worlds they know in terms of the arguments presented in the reading, and some ask students to analyze the reading in terms of specific rhetorical techniques or lines of argument. In most cases, students should have done the reading already and perhaps answered one or more of the questions that follow it. With some modification, however, many of the questions could work well as prereading exercises to get students thinking about a topic or to explore their preconceptions. If your class is small, everyone can participate in a single discussion. You may, however, wish to break the class into small groups to maximize the speaking opportunities for every student. Be sure to save some time at the end of the session for groups to summarize their discussion for the whole class (this is great practice in summarizing and constructing oral arguments). If your class periods are sufficiently long, give groups 10 or 15 minutes to prepare a discussion, and select one group to present its arguments and ideas to the class (for 5 or 10 minutes). As an additional reinforcement, the other students can analyze and discuss the rhetorical techniques used in the group's presentation. If you retain the same groups over several discussion sessions, each group could have a turn at presenting its arguments to the entire class.

Instructor's Notes

Everything's an Argument
with Readings

CHAPTER 1

Everything Is an Argument

This chapter asks students to think in new ways about the reading and writing that they do in a variety of situations. *Everything's an Argument* presents an extended argument for the idea that all language is a form of motivated action, an idea that may not make sense to many first-year students. Even confident and experienced writers will find new ideas in this chapter, and for many students these unfamiliar ideas may make for something of a conceptual mess. Give yourself and the students a few weeks to use the terminology, practice analyzing texts, and ask questions.

The most important lesson in this chapter is that all language and even images can serve as argument. Some first-year students have difficulty understanding *argument* as anything but "disagreement," and getting them to accept the word as meaning "making a point" or "reasoned inquiry" can take some time. Students may also have some difficulty making the distinction between *argument* and *persuasion*. As an in-class activity, you might ask your students to write a one-sentence definition of one of the terms. Then have students read their definitions aloud without identifying the term. The rest of the class can try to guess which word is being defined and explain their guesses.

A second important lesson in this chapter is that rhetorical situations vary widely, ranging from the obviously persuasive (the senator's defense of Homeland Security to the irate C-SPAN caller) to the poetic (Michael Lassell's poem about a brother's death). Understanding how arguments change depending on contexts and even understanding the contexts themselves can be challenging for students. Fortunately, even seemingly homogeneous classes usually are composed of students who carry different assumptions and who have varied cultural backgrounds and experiences. Have students practice analyzing arguments in class, and they'll probably encounter a broad range of knowledge, assumptions, and interpretations.

Stasis theory and the rhetorical appeals of ethos, pathos, and logos are powerful tools for understanding and creating arguments, but it may take students some time to sort them out. Students often rightly perceive the difficulty of separating the three appeals and treating them as distinct entities. In almost all rhetorical situations, the three appeals overlap significantly, so that, for example, an effective logical or emotional appeal builds a particular kind of ethos. They will also quickly realize that it can be difficult to find pure examples of the kinds of arguments that stasis theory introduces, but with work they should be able to see that many authors move through one or more stasis questions in making their arguments.

To help students understand stasis theory, you might consider walking through an imaginary crime in class. If someone goes missing, for example, there is a question of fact. Did something happen to this person? If a dead body is found, then investigators know that something happened and try to define the event: was it suicide, an accident, or a murder? If they can define the crime as murder, they might next evaluate it: was it murder in the first, second, or third degree? When they have evaluated the severity of the crime, the investigators or the judicial system makes a proposal about what to do next: should the criminal be given a prison sentence of a limited number of years, life imprisonment, or the death penalty?

Not Just Words

In this short exercise, students will interpret visual rhetoric, and the second bumper sticker offers an opportunity for thinking about how much an argument depends on the audience's preconceptions. Ask students to reread Christopher Hitchens's consideration of the word "cowboy" on page 24. Do they feel the word has positive or negative connotations? Do their feelings about the word affect how they understand the rhetoric of the second bumper sticker? Is it possible to interpret that visual argument as a criticism of George W. Bush *and* as an endorsement of him?

Exercises

1. Can an argument really be any text that expresses a point of view? What kinds of arguments — if any — might be made by the following items?

    *   the embossed leather cover of a prayer book [**An expensive embossed leather cover might suggest that the text is held in high regard, arguing that the text deserves respect and attention.**]
    *   a Boston Red Sox cap [**The cap can assert a fan's support for a baseball team and affirm a sense of identity with other fans, a city, even a region of the country. It could also be a taunt to fans of other teams, particularly the New York Yankees. It might also support the loyal tradition of Red Sox fans or celebrate their 2004 World Series win.**]
    *   a Livestrong bracelet [**The bracelet may argue that the wearer is committed to cancer-research charities or to fashionable trends.**]
    *   the label on a best-selling rap CD [**A label affixed to the CD might warn that the lyrics and themes in the album are unsuitable for children. Some people might avoid the CD for that reason, and others might select it because of the adult content.**]
    *   the health warning on a pack of cigarettes [**The warning describes potential consequences of smoking; some consumers might decide not to buy the cigarettes as a result, and some might feel guilty about their purchase. This warning might also serve as a good example of a strong argument that nonetheless frequently fails to persuade.**]
    *   a belated birthday card [**Such a card, often humorous, is frequently a plea for forgiveness or understanding, arguing that the sender deserves credit for remembering the birthday at all.**]
    *   the nutrition label on a can of soup [**The label offers facts about the product that readers may interpret as an argument for or against buying it. For example, the calories or fat or sodium totals might be higher or lower than those of competing products.**]

- the cover of a science fiction novel [**The cover usually depicts a futuristic scene. The argument might be "buy me and learn more."**]
- a colored ribbon pinned to a shirt lapel [**The ribbon may suggest that the wearer holds certain values about politics — or fashion.**]
- a Rolex watch [**The watch might imply that the owner is wealthy and tasteful enough to select a much admired, highly refined product, or it might argue that the owner wants to display his or her wealth as a mark of personal distinction.**]

2. This exercise would work well in class, perhaps as an introductory activity for the first day or two of the course. You might think about saving the responses and returning them on the last day of the class to show students how their understanding of argument has changed.

3. This exercise introduces students to one method of categorizing arguments. You could supplement this exercise by asking students to develop their own rhetorical taxonomy: how else might they divide the world of argument?

4. What common experiences — if any — do the following objects, brand names, and symbols evoke, and for what audiences in particular?

- a USDA organic label [**Associated with healthy, environmentally friendly, and perhaps fresher-tasting food; for health-conscious consumers**]
- the Nike swoosh [**Associated with athletes and athleticism, commercialization, coolness, foreign factories; probably for youths and young adults, in particular, but also for athletic older consumers**]
- the golden arches [**Associated with fast and relatively inexpensive food, convenience, efficiency, commercialism, American cultural imperialism, obesity; for children and families, perhaps travelers**]
- the Sean Jean label, as seen on its Web site [**Associated with urban style and hip-hop culture; for young, fashion-conscious consumers, particularly African Americans**]
- a can of Coca-Cola [**Associated with refreshment, relaxation, tradition, the necessity of caffeine, holidays, even U.S. power and cultural hegemony; for a worldwide audience**]

- Sleeping Beauty's castle on the Disney logo **[Associated with childhood stories, wonder, magic, entertainment, Florida vacations, corporate power; for children and families, with an especially nostalgic appeal to adults]**
- Oprah Winfrey **[Associated with sensitivity, self-empowerment, success, generosity, perhaps emotional manipulation; particularly successful with women audiences but with a broad American appeal]**
- the Vietnam Veterans Memorial **[Associated with a divisive war, the honor accorded those killed in the war, and attempts to help heal the divisions created by the war; for those close to soldiers who died and for the country at large]**
- Ground Zero **[Associated with tragedy, loss, heroism, resilience; for those who lost a loved one on 9/11 and for the country at large]**
- a dollar bill **[Associated with U.S. government, capitalism, enterprise, fiscal stability, aspiration, greed; for Americans but also some other nationalities, who may see the dollar as a threat from U.S. power or as a symbol of opportunity and success]**

5. Read the main editorial in your campus newspaper for three or four days. Then choose the most interesting one, and consider how the editor creates credibility, or ethos, in the editorial. **[Answers will vary. If your school lacks a daily student paper, you might consider having students select editorials from a variety of publications, making sure that some students choose editorials from publications targeted toward young readers, women readers, men readers, or a specialized audience. Students can then discuss how authors use different strategies for creating ethos. For example, an editorial writer in a music magazine directed toward young readers will employ ethos-building strategies significantly different from those an editorialist for the *Wall Street Journal* would use.]**

6. Take a look at the bumper sticker below, and then analyze it. What is its purpose? What kind of argument is it? Which of the stasis questions does it most appropriately respond to? What appeals does it make to its readers, and how? **[This bumper sticker makes an appeal to values by asking us to think carefully about how we define patriotism and how the choice of**

what we drive has larger effects. Encourage your students to think about the ethos of a person who might put this bumper sticker on a car and the ways that images and words make its argument.]

●●● i•claim: VISUALIZING ARGUMENT (CD-ROM)
●●● TUTORIAL 01: ARGUMENTS MAKE CLAIMS

The first chapter introduces many new concepts, and the i*Claim CD-ROM gives students the opportunity to practice applying the terminology they have learned. The first two tutorials complement this chapter especially well.

Tutorial 1, "Arguments Make Claims," offers students the chance to practice interpreting written, spoken, and visual claims. If you are able to play the CD in class, you might present the speeches by Lou Gehrig, Jesse Jackson, and Christopher Reeve from the "Arguments" section of the CD and ask students to explain the ethos of each speaker. You might also ask them to compare and contrast the contexts and the claims of the speeches. (The first tutorial includes commentary on and questions about Gehrig's speech, so take students through that tutorial before beginning the comparison exercise.)

CHAPTER 2

Arguments from the Heart—*Pathos*

The "conceptual mess" of argument and persuasion that we discussed in Chapter 1 grows messier here: if argument is primarily a form of reasoned inquiry, what is the role of emotion in a responsible argument? Students will certainly struggle, as we all do, with distinguishing between appropriate and inappropriate emotion since that distinction is determined by the rhetorical situation, especially the audience. Determining appropriate and inappropriate emotion requires judgment, and agreement is never guaranteed.

Students may also struggle with distinguishing between reason and emotion. This chapter includes excerpts from emotionally grounded arguments that are effective *because* they exist on the shifting border between emotion and reason (think of how Georgiana Kleege uses the fact of her blindness to make an emotional appeal) (page 52). You can help your students see the relationships among reason, emotion, argument, and persuasion by drawing on the board a diagram that shows rational argument as a subset of persuasion. Invite your students to help you develop another diagram that shows *everything* as an argument.

Such a diagram leaves room for emotional appeals as a legitimate part of argument and inquiry, an idea that some students resist. Before you show the diagram, though, you might have your students develop their own diagrams to illustrate the relationships. Have the class critique those student diagrams as tests: where, for example, do the civil rights arguments of Martin Luther King Jr. fit in? How about Steve Jobs's appeals to a commencement audience? Under what conditions do these and other examples serve as legitimate argument?

Exercises

1. To what specific feelings or emotions do the following slogans, sales pitches, and maxims appeal?
   - "Just do it." (ad for Nike) **[Appeal to pleasure, boldness]**

Not Just Words

This image of the flag with corporate logos in place of the stars may strike many students as offensive, but they may not be able to articulate exactly why. First make sure that they can explain what argument the image is making. Many college students are not familiar with protests against corporate power, and the purpose of the image may confuse them.

If the students are bothered by this flag, press them to discuss what makes this image troubling for them: what values and emotions does this particular representation of the flag challenge? You can extend the consideration of this image by discussing whether appropriating an image like the flag is ever appropriate for protest or for support. How could they adapt the imagery of the flag to express their opinions about the United States?

- "Think different." (ad for Apple computers) **[Appeal to pride, creativity]**
- "Reach out and touch someone." (ad for AT&T) **[Appeal to love, joy, and pleasure]**
- "In your heart, you know he's right." (1964 campaign slogan for U.S. presidential candidate Barry Goldwater, a conservative) **[Appeal to empathy]**
- "It's the economy, stupid!" (1992 campaign theme for U.S. presidential candidate Bill Clinton) **[Appeal to fear or alienation]**
- "By any means necessary." (rallying cry from Malcolm X) **[Appeal to fear or anxiety]**
- "Have it your way." (slogan for Burger King) **[Appeal to freedom, pleasure]**
- "You can trust your car to the man who wears the star." (slogan for Texaco) **[Appeal to anxiety and attachment]**
- "It's everywhere you want to be." (slogan for Visa) **[Appeal to pleasure, anxiety, or security]**
- "Know what comes between me and my Calvins? Nothing!" (tag line for Calvin Klein jeans) **[Appeal to pleasure]**

- "Don't mess with Texas!" (antilitter campaign slogan) **[Appeal to fear and empathy]**

2–4. Most students can readily appreciate the connections between rhetoric and advertising, so asking them to determine how advertising employs rhetorical strategies can be an especially productive exercise. You might emphasize how different advertisers focus on different emotions. A magazine like *Rolling Stone*, aimed at a younger demographic than *Time*, is more likely to contain humorous advertisements. Ads in *Time* and *Newsweek* might appeal to the emotions that parents feel about their children since those magazines have an older audience.

If you'd like to examine the use of arguments from the heart over a longer period of time, you might ask students to do some research. Ask them to find texts of powerful speeches, such as Pericles's Funeral Oration, Martin Luther King Jr.'s "I Have a Dream," or Ronald Reagan's State of the Union addresses. Ask students to identify the emotional appeals *and* the logical appeals and to explain their combined effectiveness.

●●● i·claim: VISUALIZING ARGUMENT (CD-ROM)
●●● ARGUMENTS: APPEALS TO PATHOS

If you've already played students the speeches by Jackson, Reeve, and Gehrig that were mentioned in the notes for Chapter 1, you might review those speeches in light of the new information about emotional appeals in this chapter. How does emotion work in these moments? In particular, how do Jackson and Reeve use arguments from the heart to help bolster their claims of reason?

If you can use the disc in class, a good group-work assignment would be to ask pairs of students to sort the "Arguments" section for "Appeals to Pathos." Have each small group pick three or four of the arguments and explain how each argument appeals to pathos. Some of these—the container of I Can't Believe It's Not Butter, for example—might be hard for them to explain at first, but working together they should be able to articulate the appeals. You might also ask students to complete this kind of analysis as a homework assignment; separating the appeals to pathos from the other elements of argument will force them to sharpen their thinking about how rhetoric works.

CHAPTER 3

Arguments Based on Character—*Ethos*

Aristotle says in the *Rhetoric* that the most important of the three proofs (logical, pathetic, ethical) is the argument based on character: if the audience does not trust the orator, all else is in vain.

This chapter presents two primary difficulties for students. First, many students feel uncomfortable with the idea that ethos is context-specific. They do not like the idea that good and honorable people can seek to change their self-presentation for different audiences without lying or misrepresenting themselves. Further, the idea that, say, Jessica Simpson has a more credible ethos than a senator or governor in the right context—for example, a cosmetics advertisement— bothers some students. Once they grasp the idea that context determines an argument's success, this idea that ethos can be elastic makes more sense.

The second and more important difficulty is that some first-year students find it a challenge to take on a voice they are not accustomed to and call it their own. Many students simply do not have the writing experience to believe that they have more than one voice or that they could develop a variety of voices for different rhetorical contexts. Some students will want to argue that adopting different voices is a form of lying—by creating characters that do not exist or by taking on authority that is not theirs to claim.

Explain to students that the written voices they use in class, in emails to family members, and in job applications, for example, already differ but that they are not necessarily false representations. Instead, each of these three kinds of writing attempts to create a character who foregrounds certain elements of students' interests and expertise and backgrounds others.

Not Just Words

This visual argument might be even more effective if you have students go to the Swift Vets' Web site at <http://www.swiftvets.com/index.php> to see the picture change in its original context. This image from a 2004 presidential campaign may not be meaningful to students, but adapting the strategy to their own arguments would be a great exercise for small groups, allowing students to produce their own arguments and enhance their technical skills (if they work on a Web site). Have your students present their work to the whole class, and be sure to press them to specify their audience(s). Different audiences require different kinds of authority, and a project like this can help students grasp that essential principle.

Exercises

1. Consider the ethos of each of the following public figures. Then describe one or two public arguments, campaigns, or products that might benefit from their endorsements as well as several that would not. **[Answers will vary; some suggestions are provided.]**

   - Oprah Winfrey — TV celebrity **[The popular host appeals especially to women, but her appeal is probably as broad as anyone's in America; her caring, generous, trustworthy demeanor means that she could sell almost anything and could have serious political influence as well.]**
   - Ellen Degeneres — comedian and talk-show host **[The warm and funny host has fairly broad appeal and could sell many products, particularly to women; because of her identification with gay rights, she might not be popular with conservative audiences.]**
   - Dick Cheney — vice president **[The long-time government insider has great appeal in conservative circles; some audiences — especially Democratic and liberal ones —**

view him with great suspicion as wielding power behind the scenes; he could endorse products for older, more conservative Americans.]

- Katie Holmes — actress [**The sweet but feisty young actress's upcoming marriage to Tom Cruise might suggest a certain strength of character; she might pitch "stay in school" campaigns and sell clothing, fashion, and cosmetics to young women; she is not likely to be a spokesperson for products aimed at older people.**]
- Colin Powell — former secretary of state in the Bush administration [**The highly respected military and political leader has stature as a sober, mature, and experienced leader, which might lead to selling insurance or investments; he probably would not sell everyday consumer goods like laundry detergent; he might be very successful as a spokesperson for civic or educational initiatives.**]
- Al Sharpton — civil rights activist and politician [**The brash, outspoken, left-wing leader is a strong advocate for liberal causes; he probably would be a good pitchman for "get out the vote," education, and African American issues, though he could be potentially divisive in many contexts.**]
- Queen Latifah — actress and rap artist [**The funny, empathetic figure appeals especially to women; she has already sold makeup and pizza and been connected to Wal-Mart.**]
- Dave Chapelle — humorist and columnist [**The edgy comedian includes plenty of pointed social and political satire in his show, as well as some drug humor; he probably should not sell serious products like life insurance but has enormous appeal to young audiences.**]
- Jeff Gordon — NASCAR champion [**The highly successful, photogenic NASCAR racer is controversial because he's a non-Southerner in a heavily Southern sport and because he looks less masculine than most NASCAR drivers; he could (and does) sell many products such as milk, Pepsi, and car-related products; he probably has little clout in political campaigns but might work as a spokesperson for worthy causes.**]
- Barbara Boxer — U.S. senator from California [**The outspoken liberal senator seems to be a polarizing figure; she**

would have great appeal to and great clout with liberal and progressive audiences but little success with conservative ones.]

- Bill O'Reilly—TV news commentator [**The aggressive, opinionated talk-show host works for the Fox News Channel; he usually advocates conservative causes with appeals to a blue-collar background and populist ethos; he probably should not endorse luxury goods or products that might seem frivolous.**]

- Marge Simpson—sensible wife and mother on *The Simpsons* [**The generally responsible cartoon housewife occasionally goes off the deep end and often appears naïve; she could be an advocate for any number of mainstream products but is not likely to represent upscale or serious (e.g., life insurance) products.**]

2–4. The strategies we outline in this chapter (claiming authority and establishing credibility) work in almost any rhetorical situation, and we have included excerpts that demonstrate the importance of arguments from character. You can extend the exercises by asking students to list the many voices they have and the situations in which they are appropriate. Ask students to find things they have written for different audiences, or assign them a topic and a set of audiences. For example, have them write three emails announcing that they've been dismissed from school. How is it different to write this news to one's parents, one's best friend, one's high school teachers, one's siblings? (Note that this assignment asks most students to assume a voice they can't imagine actually needing to assume.) Once they've written their samples, ask the students to find and annotate the textual cues that demonstrate shifting rhetorical ethos.

●●● i·cite: VISUALIZING SOURCES (CD-ROM)
●●● TUTORIAL 02: SOURCES ARE PEOPLE TALKING TO EACH OTHER
    TUTORIAL 03: SOURCES HAVE AN AGENDA

The i*Cite CD contains Tutorial 3, "Sources Have an Agenda," which is also an argument that sources have an ethos. A writer who researches also has an ethos—one that is based in part on which sources the author uses and in part on how the author uses the sources. Have your students also go through Tutorial 2, "Sources Are People Talking to Each Other." This tutorial helps students understand that sources (and those who write arguments using sources) exist in a larger context that can help them determine what kind of ethos the author has. As mentioned in the above notes, the context of the argument determines what kind of ethos is necessary for the occasion.

●●● i·claim: VISUALIZING ARGUMENT (CD-ROM)
●●● ARGUMENTS: APPEALS TO ETHOS

On the i*Claim CD, have students sort "Arguments" for "Appeals to Ethos." You might have students discuss their views of the ethos of some of the individuals in this section and have them consider the particular context in which the argument is presented. Many students might already have an opinion about Lance Armstrong. Does their opinion of Armstrong change any if they see him on the cover of *Every Second Counts?* What about Jackie Chan? Does he have a viable ethos for a milk advertisement? As group work or a homework assignment, have students consider how ethos figures into an argument in which no person is visible. How can a newspaper have an ethos? What ethos does the *New York Times* have?

CHAPTER 4

Arguments Based on Facts and Reason—*Logos*

Finally, the good stuff: evidence, facts, testimony, statistics—real numbers, real facts, and no more opinions and feelings. That's the attitude some first-year student writers will take. Students who feel lost without "solid facts" to support arguments will be happy to come to this chapter. But using evidence responsibly is complicated. Students will need to become comfortable critiquing facts as well as opinions, questioning surveys and statistical evidence, and uncovering assumptions that lie behind enthymemes. For example, you might introduce the factual claim that the Bayer company used to use in its aspirin advertising: "Nothing works better than Bayer." It's a fact: no aspirin works better than Bayer aspirin. But it's a fact that conceals the important point that other aspirins work equally well.

The concept of the arguable proposition might help students see that making a distinction between fact and opinion can sometimes be difficult. Certain propositions are not arguable: the square root of 81 is 9; Spain borders Portugal; Charles Dickens wrote in English. We do not argue about these claims because we accept them as commonplaces: they are, for most purposes, facts. But other facts are arguable: Christopher Columbus discovered America, William Shakespeare wrote all the plays attributed to him, clear-cutting in the rain forest has little environmental impact. At some point in the not too distant past, these last three facts were commonplaces, at least to certain audiences. But now they are arguable propositions: reasonable people could dispute the claims and offer other evidence in support of counterarguments.

Your students will be able to discuss this image more effectively if you send them to the Web site at <http://www.protestwarrior .com/signs.php?thumb=1> to view the image in its original context. They will need to click through a gallery of posters that use many of the same tactics to find the one printed here. Ask your students to read the mission statement on the Web site to further understand the context within which this image was created. Depending on the makeup of your classroom, this image might generate heated conversation and opinions from all sides of the political spectrum. It will help if you keep the focus on the visual and verbal strategies employed here. A good place to start might be to break your class up into small groups and ask them to discuss how the text is subverted by the image. How does the image undermine the statement: "Liberating Iraqi Children from Tyanny/It's Costing Too Much!"? How does the image appeal to emotions? Have them report back to the class with their findings.

Exercises

1. Discuss whether the following statements are examples of hard evidence **[inartistic]** or rational appeals **[artistic]**. Not all cases are clear-cut.
    - "The bigger they are, the harder they fall." **[Artistic]**
    - Drunk drivers are involved in more than 50 percent of traffic deaths. **[Inartistic; ask students to discuss how the word "involved" works in this claim.]**
    - DNA tests of skin found under the victim's fingernails suggest that the defendant was responsible for the assault. **[Inartistic]**
    - Polls suggest that a large majority of Americans favor a constitutional amendment to ban flag burning. **[Inartistic]**
    - A psychologist testified that teenage violence could not be blamed on computer games. **[Inartistic]**
    - Honey attracts more flies than vinegar. **[Artistic]**
    - History proves that cutting tax rates increases government rev-

enues because people work harder when they can keep more of what they earn. **[Both]**

- "We have nothing to fear but fear itself." **[Artistic]**
- Air bags ought to be removed from vehicles because they can kill young children and small-framed adults. **[Inartistic]**

2–4. This chapter distinguishes between artistic and inartistic proofs: the first relies on authorial invention (enthymemes, syllogisms, analogies, and so on), and the second on specific pieces of evidence. Our experience has been that first-year writers are drawn to the inartistic appeals out of a belief that nothing convinces like hard evidence—the "facts" that seem inarguable. You will need to help your students see the effectiveness of artistic appeals, too. We offer several excerpts that you could use to explore artistic appeals, but a quick look at any newspaper op-ed page will reveal many more examples. As an introduction to Toulmin logic and as evidence for the idea that artistic appeals can be effective, have your students find the claims and reasons embedded in newspaper editorials. Student newspapers also offer, in our experience, examples of *ineffective* artistic appeals. First-year writers are usually able to explain what has gone wrong in an unpersuasive opinion piece, and you could profitably steer class discussion to the author's use of evidence.

●●● **i·claim:** VISUALIZING ARGUMENT (CD-ROM)
●●● TUTORIAL 06: ARGUMENTS USE LOGIC

Tutorial 6, "Arguments Use Logic," on the i*Claim CD offers a thorough introduction to how arguments use logic or logical fallacies. Students are often especially interested in logical fallacies, and the assignment in which they rewrite the headline for the shampoo ad will help them think about why some people intentionally choose to use logical fallacies. In what contexts is a fallacy more effective than a rigorously argued logical claim?

The "Arguments" section is once again invaluable. Have students sort the arguments for "Appeals to Logos." They will quickly notice that many of these arguments do not use logos as their primary appeal. In those cases, what role do facts and reason play? Ask your students to examine at least twelve of the sample arguments. Can they generalize about the kinds of situations that benefit most from logical appeals?

CHAPTER 5

Thinking Rhetorically

This chapter puts together many principles from earlier chapters and asks students to use those principles as analytical tools. (The next few chapters emphasize how rhetoric can help them produce arguments.) The rhetorical concepts that the book has introduced help students to understand how and why people make the arguments that they do.

First-year writers, who bring a range of experiences and abilities to the classroom, may know some of these concepts under different names. "Making a claim," for example, could be the equivalent of "writing a thesis." "Giving an argument shape" might be understood as "organizing." Students probably also can make sense of the differences between claims of value, emotion, character, and fact: they see such claims every day, and learning to think rhetorically can be understood as a way of organizing and commenting on ideas that they intuitively grasp. But once they can articulate these ideas, they can think, read, and write more consciously and critically.

Encourage your students to explore their familiarity with these concepts by asking them to name examples of each of the categories of argument. Popular advertisements are a good tool for showing students the power of carefully crafted appeals; students have sometimes studied advertisements in psychology classes, and they come to think of advertising as a series of tricks. But rhetorical analysis can help them see advertising—and therefore many other forms of discourse—as communication that they can understand. And what they can understand in others' arguments they can apply to their own.

Exercises

1. Describe a persuasive moment you can recall from a speech, an article, an editorial, an advertisement, or your personal experience. Alternatively, research one of the following famous moments of persuasion and then describe the circumstances of the appeal: what the historical situation was, what issues were at

This exercise helps reveal how powerful a rhetorical analysis can be. Some students may feel energized by the idea that they can discover hidden agendas through the application of rhetorical concepts.

It's worth discussing the effectiveness of the claims made by <Zombietime.com> and by the *San Francisco Chronicle.* Is Zombietime right that this picture reveals an "insidious" bias? And is the *Chronicle* really addressing the quality of its ethos, which is what Zombietime ultimately attacks? A careful discussion of the sample should help students make their own arguments about the images that they find.

Students are frequently adept at reading visual arguments, but they haven't had much practice paying attention to individual elements of argument inside those texts. Having students present their rhetorical analysis of the photo to the class will force them to articulate how they broke the text down into individual elements.

stake, what the purpose of the address was, and what made the particular speech memorable.

- Abraham Lincoln's "Gettysburg Address" (1863) **[The turning point of the American Civil War, a reaffirmation of core Union values]**
- Elizabeth Cady Stanton's draft of the "Declaration of Sentiments" for the Seneca Falls Convention (1848) **[A key statement of principles and arguments for women's rights]**
- Franklin Roosevelt's inaugural address (1933) **[An attempt by a new president to give Americans hope during the Great Depression]**
- Winston Churchill's addresses to the British people during the early stages of World War II (1940) **[An attempt to rally a nation against a Nazi military onslaught threatening Britain]**
- Martin Luther King Jr.'s "Letter from Birmingham Jail" (1963) **[An attempt to remind white Christian leaders of the religious roots of the civil rights movement and to defend the principles of nonviolent civil disobedience]**

- Ronald Reagan's tribute to the *Challenger* astronauts (1986) **[A eulogy for the astronauts killed in the explosion of the space shuttle and an argument for continuing space exploration]**
- Toni Morrison's speech accepting the Nobel Prize (1993) **[An assertion of a feminist, African American presence in literature and theory]**
- George Bush's speech to Congress following the 9/11 terrorist attacks (2001) **[An argument for resolve in the face of danger, an affirmation of American values and strength, and a warning to terrorist groups and other governments]**

2–5. These exercises ask a great deal of students and could easily serve as paper assignments. One of the most difficult aspects of a rhetorical analysis is that after students work hard to pull apart the different aspects of an argument, they're asked to put them all back together. Make sure that your students choose clearly argumentative texts to analyze. Though it's certainly possible to present an excellent rhetorical analysis of a news article, that may be a more challenging assignment than most first-year writing students should take on for their first rhetorical analysis. You might consider taking any one of these exercises and modeling the response for your classes to help build their confidence before they begin their own rhetorical analyses.

●●● i·claim: VISUALIZING ARGUMENT (CD-ROM)
●●● TUTORIAL 03: ARGUMENTS HAVE GOALS

Because this chapter asks students to apply so many new concepts, they can find it to be one of the most challenging chapters in the book. Tutorial 3, "Arguments Have Goals," is a valuable complement to this chapter. When students write a rhetorical analysis, they frequently become so concerned with breaking the argument apart to isolate separate elements that they overlook the purpose of the argument. A rhetorical analysis that recognizes the goals of an argument can identify why the creator of the argument makes certain choices, including choices to omit, for example, a reliance on logical claims. Tutorial 3 will help keep students focused on judging how well the argument they are analyzing accomplishes its goals.

CHAPTER 6

Structuring Arguments

Toulmin logic can seem complicated at first — so many concepts, so many terms. But for reasons that we explain in the chapter, Toulmin logic can also be a powerful as an analytic and productive tool. Our experience has been that when first-year students commit themselves to understanding and using the Toulmin framework, their writing improves noticeably. Students begin to make arguments that use evidence effectively, and they write papers that show greater sensitivity to audience. The system holds students accountable for every part of their argument, while forcing them to question the foundations and assumptions underlying their claims.

But like any complicated system, Toulmin logic takes time to learn. Do not expect your students to become comfortable with the concepts immediately. Instead, plan to introduce and review the various elements of Toulmin argument over a period of weeks. This chapter explains the system in a few pages, but the material is significantly more complex than that of the previous chapters. Take your time leading students through the idea of claims and reasons. These two key elements might take a week to explain completely, especially if you use real-world examples in which claims and reasons are not made explicit. (Letters to the editor of any newspaper will illustrate the problems of making clear claims supported by coherent reasons. Some letters will serve as examples of good, clear writing; others will make great counterexamples.)

Students usually struggle with the idea that there are two kinds of evidence — in support of reasons and of warrants — and that an argument might be exemplary in its use of one while completely ignoring the other. The Toulmin system gives you a way of explaining to your students exactly what the evidentiary problems are in their arguments. You can praise a student's use of statistical evidence in support of the reasons, for instance, while asking him or her to provide more evidence in support of the warrant. Our experience has been that when students come to understand the distinction between these two

Not Just Words

This exercise asks students to think carefully about document design. They already respond to the layout of text even if they don't realize it. Almost all students react positively to seeing pages of quick dialogue in an assigned novel; the visual cues of short bursts of text indicate that they'll get through the assignment more quickly. Show them pages filled with long paragraphs that reach all the margins on the page, and their eyes will give them plenty of information before they start reading. If you can access the Web in class, you might show students images of newspaper front pages from the early twentieth century beside current front pages of *USA Today*. The importance of white space will be immediately clear to them. After comparing images from different time periods, have them make up their own announcements about a July 4th celebration.

forms of evidence, they also learn to create more effective enthymemes: students can work backward from evidence to claims.

Exercises

1. Following is a claim followed by five possible supporting reasons. State the warrant that would support each of the arguments in brief. Which of the warrants would need to be defended? Which would a college audience likely accept without significant backing? **[Answers will vary; some suggested warrants are offered.]**

    We should amend the Constitution to abolish the Electoral College

    • because a true democracy is based on the popular vote, not the votes of the usually unknown electors. **[True democracy should be our goal; true democracy does not rely on representatives to do the people's voting.]**

    • because under the Electoral College system the votes of people who have minority opinions in some states end up not counting. **[Minority opinions should count in every state; all votes should count equally.]**

- because then Al Gore would have won the 2000 election. **[Al Gore would be a better president than George W. Bush; Al Gore should have won the 2000 election.]**
- because the Electoral College is an outdated relic of an age when the political leaders didn't trust the people. **[Outdated institutions need to be changed; political leaders should trust the people who vote.]**
- because the Electoral College skews power toward small and mid-size states for no good reason. **[The Electoral College disrupts the natural balance of power; there must be a good reason if power is going to be skewed power toward small and mid-size states.]**

2–5. You can help students learn Toulmin logic by taking every opportunity to use the terminology in class. The more students hear the words, the more comfortable they will be using them themselves. (We have gone so far sometimes as to state *everything* in class as claim, reasons, and warrant: "Claim: Rob, you should help me arrange the desks in a circle. Reason: Because I want everyone to see each other in the discussion. Warrant: Seeing other students in a discussion is good. Warrant: If I want a student to do something in class, the student should do it." Or if a student says she is hungry, we restate it: "Claim: I am hungry. Reason: Because I have not eaten since last night.") Some students might complain about the complicated system. Help these students make their complaints using Toulmin logic: "Claim: I do not like learning Toulmin logic. Reason: Toulmin is too complicated." You can examine these claims, explore the reasons and warrants, and show your students why Toulmin will help them. In short, use the system to show how powerful it can be.

A final note: students work hard in other classes to learn complicated systems. Every academic field has terminology and a taxonomy that take time to learn. You should make no apologies for teaching difficult material. Toulmin is hard to learn, but the effort is repaid many times over. (Enthymeme: If students work hard to learn in any other classes, then they can expect to work hard to learn in a writing class, too.)

●●● **i•claim:** VISUALIZING ARGUMENT (CD-ROM)
●●● TUTORIAL 04: ARGUMENTS USE SUPPORT

Though it doesn't reinforce Toulmin terminology, Tutorial 4, "Arguments Use Support," usefully complements this chapter. You might find it productive to ask students to examine the support that this tutorial introduces and explain how Toulmin terminology helps make sense of evidence. Students who then might need some extra reinforcement with Toulmin terminology should consult the "Glossary" section of i*Claim.

CHAPTER 7

Arguments of Fact

This is the first chapter that deals explicitly with the stases that were introduced in Chapter 1. The first stasis question in the ancients' tradition was of fact: did something happen? Before an argument can progress to the next stage, everyone must agree that something did happen. Consider a missing person case. If no one knows where the person is and no body can be found, then authorities cannot arrest and try someone for murder, decide that an accident occurred, or rule the death a suicide. First, there must be agreement that something happened; only after the parties have agreed that *something* has happened can they determine which term or definition best applies. An argument of fact is the basis of further claims.

Your students may find arguments of fact to be especially interesting because they have long understood facts to be immutable. Problems arise, however, when they begin to consider what kinds of facts can be reasonably argued and which cannot be reasonably argued. There's no easy answer to this question. For instance, in the exercises for this chapter, the statement that there has only been one Roman Catholic president of the first forty-three hardly seems arguable. A quick look in any encyclopedia would confirm this fact. But what if a historian found evidence that an earlier president was a Roman Catholic who had suppressed his religious affiliation because he feared the anti-Catholic prejudice that was common in the late nineteenth century? In that case, even this seemingly straightforward, easily verified claim becomes arguable. A good argument with good evidence can make new facts.

This example, which will fall far afield from the work that students will produce in their classes, nonetheless might help them understand that facts can be arguable. They may, however, find it difficult to come up with topics of their own that are manageable in the papers they'll be writing for class. Research will play a crucial role in developing good factual arguments, and the brainstorming exercises included below should help them sort out which arguments would be particularly viable for a paper.

Not Just Words

The visual presentation of information in graphs and charts asks students to read in a different way. To extend this exercise, you might ask students to find examples of arguments made visually that mislead the viewer. You might also spend some time looking at the different graphs that appear in *USA Today*. You might then have the students compare those graphs to the mock graphics that the satirical newspaper *The Onion* <www.the onion.com> includes on its front page.

Exercises

1. For each topic in the following list, decide whether the claim is worth arguing to a college audience and explain why or why not: **[Answers will vary; some suggestions are provided.]**
    *   Hurricanes are increasing in number and ferocity. **[Worth arguing; how far back does reliable data reach? How well can we measure hurricane strength before the Saffir-Simpson scale was created? How do we compare hurricanes that are now hitting populated coastal areas to those that hit coastal areas with few residents?]**
    *   Many people die annually of cancer. **[Not worth arguing; the claim can be easily supported by one or two numbers.]**
    *   Fewer people would die of heart disease each year if more of them paid attention to their diets. **[Perhaps worth arguing; though diet has long been considered a risk factor for heart disease, there might be contrary evidence.]**
    *   Japan might have come to terms more readily in 1945 if the Allies hadn't demanded unconditional surrender. **[Worth arguing]**
    *   Boys would do better in school if there were more men teaching in elementary and secondary classrooms. **[Worth arguing]**
    *   The ever-increasing number of minorities in higher education is evidence that racial problems have just about ended in the United States. **[Worth arguing]**

- There aren't enough high-paying jobs for college graduates these days. **[Worth arguing; what constitutes enough? What do we consider high pay?]**
- Hydrogen may never be a viable alternative to fossil fuels because it takes too much energy to change hydrogen into a useable form. **[Worth arguing; how much energy is too much? What if we run out of fossil fuels or if obtaining them becomes too costly?]**
- Only one of the first forty-three presidents of the United States was a Catholic. **[Not worth arguing; but see the discussion of this issue above.]**
- Political activists have grossly exaggerated the effects of the USA Patriot Act on free expression. **[Worth arguing]**

2–4. These exercises would be especially helpful for helping students brainstorm paper topics of their own. First-year writing students often find that it's difficult to come up with reasonable factual claims for short papers. You might use exercises 2 and 4 as group work in class. Immediate peer review of topic ideas will help some students see how reasonable their claims might be as well as how much work individual claims might require. Exercise 3 gives students a number of examples of factual arguments to look at as models. You might also direct them to <www.snopes.com>, a site that examines urban legends, for enjoyable examples of factual arguments.

●●● **i·cite:** VISUALIZING SOURCES (CD-ROM)
●●● TUTORIAL 03: SOURCES HAVE AN AGENDA

Factual arguments require research, and students must be able to evaluate sources effectively before they can utilize them in their arguments. Tutorial 3, "Sources Have an Agenda," on the i*Cite CD-ROM complements this chapter especially well. This tutorial helps students to see how factual sources can have an agenda and to understand that the existence of an agenda or bias (a particularly loaded word for many students) does not necessarily hurt the credibility of a source. This tutorial will also help students understand that *how* a source or a student writer uses facts is part of an argument.

CHAPTER 8

Arguments of Definition

A traditional legal example of stasis theory's practical application concerns a missing urn. This example works well in the classroom as an introduction to arguments of definition: an urn is discovered to be missing from a house and is found in the house of another man. At the level of fact, there is agreement: the defendant has the urn that belongs to the plaintiff. But there is considerable disagreement about definition: the plaintiff argues that the urn was stolen, whereas the defendant argues that it was merely *borrowed*. The case can go no further until the parties settle the question of definition. Only after the parties have defined "theft" and "borrowing" and only after they have determined which term best applies can the case move forward.

Toulmin logic will help you explain the contested — and the rhetorical — nature of definitional claims. Because definitional criteria are warrants, they must be chosen with audience in mind (if the audience members do not accept the criteria you choose, they will not accept any other part of the argument). You could return to the urn example to demonstrate the need for *shared* definitions of theft or borrowing. If, for example, you were to argue that borrowing without explicit permission constitutes theft, you would need to provide evidence for that criterion; your evidence must be tailored to a particular audience. Not everyone would accept that criterion: what about close friends who share their possessions without needing permission each time they borrow something?

Some students who struggle will be able to place an object within a given class (a fiddle is certainly a violin; prostitution is an exploitation of women; paid workers are not volunteers) but will balk at the need to explore or defend definitional criteria. Turn to Toulmin to show that they might have evidence in support of their reasons but not in support of the warrants — the definitional criteria themselves.

Not Just Words

These images may not be straightforward for some students, but the conflicting definitions that your students pull out could lead to excellent class discussions. You might extend the exercise by asking students to bring or create images that illustrate their preferred definitions of patriotism. The adaptation of the Uncle Sam recruiting poster might be an especially interesting image to ask your students to work with. How might they appropriate this image to put forward their own definition of patriotism? You can have them describe how they might put together a poster of their own, but many of your students can manipulate images to create their own poster, so you might consider asking them to bring those images into class or posting them on the Web.

Exercises

1. Briefly discuss the criteria you might use to define the italicized terms in the following controversial claims of definition. Compare your definitions of the terms with those of your classmates. [**Answers will vary; some possibilities are offered.**]
   - Graphic novels are *serious literature.* [**Must offer some psychological depth and some meaning beyond the surface; must be of high enough quality to be read for decades or centuries; must offer some kind of commentary on the human condition**]
   - Burning a nation's flag is a *hate crime.* [**Must be a crime or prosecutable act; must be aimed at a specific group; must be intended to hurt, demean, or disparage**]
   - The Bushes have become America's *royal family.* [**Must be an extended family; must have exercised political power over an extended period; must capture the imagination of the public; must bring attention to individual family members through family membership**]
   - Matt Drudge and Larry Flynt are legitimate *journalists.* [**Must earn a living by reporting the news; must be trained in journalism either by schooling or through practical**

experience; must report the news ethically and responsibly]

- College sports programs have become *big businesses*. [**Must generate considerable income; must be enterprises that aim at constant growth; must be regional or national in scope; must make decisions to ensure their own success or profit**]
- Plagiarism can be an act of *civil disobedience*. [**Must be a conscious act of law-breaking; must be an act intended to question the legitimacy of the law being broken; must be a violation with legal consequences; must be an act for which the perpetrator is willing to accept the consequences**]
- Satanism is a *religion* properly protected by the First Amendment. [**Must be a set of beliefs about the ultimate meaning or focus of life; must have beliefs that are shared by a group; must have beliefs that have a bearing on the conduct of one's life**]
- Campaign contributions are acts of *free speech*. [**Must be an expression of an idea through language, written or oral; must be an expression of a political character or with a political interest; must be noncommercial and nonthreatening**]
- The District of Columbia should have all the privileges of an American *state*. [**Must be a discrete territory in a relationship with the United States of America; must be a territory of reasonable size; must be a unit with economic and social diversity; must have historical significance as a territory**]
- Committed gay and lesbian couples should have the legal privileges of *marriage*. [**Must be an enduring bond between adults; must be a bond established to sustain family life; must be a sacramental bond; must be a sexual union**]

2–3. These exercises offer suggestions for helping students think of their own definitional claims by extending examples in the text. Another good exercise is for students to come up with far-fetched definitional claims: Oprah Winfrey is a cult leader; Disney is a virus; Tom Cruise is an alien. We've seen students write engaging, thoughtful arguments on these topics. Students often gravitate to topics such as capital punishment or abortion when writing definition arguments; however, when they approach the assignment more creatively, they seem to structure their arguments more effectively and develop their criteria in unexpected but reasonable ways. (An alien doesn't have to come from outer space, for example; maybe the world of celebrity that Tom Cruise inhabits is so different from ours that it may as well be an alien world.) When students write about the more creative claims and experiment with off-beat arguments, they have a greater opportunity to say something fresh.

●●● i•claim: VISUALIZING ARGUMENT (CD-ROM)
●●● TUTORIAL 05: ARGUMENTS CONSIDER MULTIPLE VIEWPOINTS

Definition arguments are powerful. They often establish fundamental agreements, and if an author or a speaker can convince an audience to accept his or her definition, then the rest of the argument becomes much easier. It's no wonder that students want to go for big topics like abortion and capital punishment when writing definition arguments; definitions take those large issues to their essential disagreements (if you can get an audience to agree that abortion or capital punishment is murder, it becomes much more difficult to defend those things). Because of the importance of definitions, you might pair this chapter with Tutorial 5, "Arguments Consider Multiple Viewpoints." This tutorial will help students see that good arguments aren't necessarily about scoring points over an opposing team but can be about bringing an audience around to agreement.

Because the "Arguments" section of the CD allows users to sort for "Arguments of Definition," you might ask students to look over several of the thumbnails that come up as definition arguments. For homework, ask students to identify the definition claim and the audience for the claim. What competing claims of definition can they identify, and how might they take those competing claims into account if they were writing a paper on this argument?

CHAPTER 9

Evaluations

In the notes for Chapter 8, we explained the classic illustration of the missing urn: the urn belonging to one man is found in the home of another. The parties disagree about the nature of the incident. One says the urn was stolen, and the other says it was merely borrowed. The matter is stuck at the level of definition, but let's imagine that the court decides the urn was stolen. The defendant might argue that he stole the urn for a good reason: the urn contained water that he needed for his ill child. The defendant now makes an argument of evaluation: the act of theft was, he claims, praiseworthy.

You can use the story of the urn to show your students how arguments of evaluation grow out of arguments of definition. The transition from definition to evaluation can be tricky, however; as you're writing, it's not always clear when you're defining and when you're evaluating. (For example, if you define someone as a hero, isn't that also an evaluation?) Nevertheless, most students will benefit from thinking of the two as separate, at least in the abstract.

Many students will need help choosing the level of evaluative abstraction for their arguments. It's one thing to argue that *Raiders of the Lost Ark* is great art; it's something else to argue that it's a good Harrison Ford-starring blockbuster. The best argument probably lies between those extremes, and most students will need help crafting a strong, arguable thesis. Some students will be content to argue that something is good or bad; push them to complicate their ideas so that they write more interesting arguments.

As with arguments of definition, evaluative arguments challenge students to defend their criteria. Toulmin logic will show that criteria are warrants and must be developed with audience in mind. If the audience does not accept the criteria, the evaluative judgment will not be accepted either. Peer review or other forms of draft response will provide students with an audience of thoughtful readers who might challenge writers' criteria.

Not Just Words

The power of a chart like this can perhaps best be understood like one might understand a Piet Mondrian painting: if you rearrange the given presentation, you change everything. Ask students how they might rearrange this chart. What information could they highlight or suppress? How might a supporter of the American effort in Iraq present the same information? You might ask students to research how political campaigns use charts and graphs to present information. How do they design visual information to make their arguments?

Exercises

1. Choose one item from the followings lists that you understand well enough to evaluate. Develop several criteria of evaluation you could defend to distinguish excellence from mediocrity in the area. Then choose another item from the list, this time one you do not know much about at all, and explain the research you might do to discover reasonable criteria of evaluation for it. **[Answers will vary considerably. You might use this exercise as an in-class activity, having students work in groups according to which topics they know best. Many students will be surprised by how many criteria the group can come up with and how challenging it can be to establish criteria that many people can accept.]**
    - fashion designers
    - Navajo rugs
    - musicals
    - spoken-word poetry
    - UN secretary generals
    - NFL quarterbacks
    - contemporary painters
    - TV journalists
    - TV sitcoms
    - health food
    - animated films

2–6. Exercises 2 through 5 highlight the importance of developing evaluative criteria, which in our experience has been the step that most frustrates students. Because students generally feel comfortable with evaluative arguments in some form (such as for movies and sports), they can usually generate topics and claims with ease. They tend to have more difficulty tailoring criteria to specific audiences. With supplementary exercises, therefore, we recommend that you focus on helping them think about the warrants for particular claims, a skill that they can then transfer to their papers. Exercise 6 encourages a more analytic approach to evaluation using a genre that students probably have not studied much. This exercise also helps move students from some potentially simple evaluation arguments (what makes a good pizza?) to more academic writing.

●●● **i·claim:** VISUALIZING ARGUMENT (CD-ROM)
●●● TUTORIAL 04: ARGUMENTS USE SUPPORT

Evaluation arguments are common, so students often find them easier to write than other sorts of arguments. But evaluations in an academic context ask students to find reasons for their opinions; they can't just say "I like it" or "I don't like it" and stop. We stress the importance of finding good evaluative criteria above, and Tutorial 4, "Arguments Use Support," works well with this chapter. With this argument more than any other, students need to be reminded of the importance of supporting their arguments so that their target audiences will find their claims persuasive.

Because the "Arguments" section of the CD allows students to sort for "Arguments of Evaluation," you might ask students to look over several of the thumbnails that come up as evaluation arguments. For homework, ask students to identify the evaluative claim and the audience for the claim. What are the implied criteria for evaluation?

CHAPTER 10

Causal Arguments

Causal arguments can be extremely challenging for students; the logic of causality is complex, the evidence is often shaky, and the results can be uncertain. The guide to writing causal argument in the chapter can help walk students through the process of writing a causal argument.

In some versions of the stases, causal arguments came before arguments of evaluation; in others, they came after. Show your class (by using the examples from this book or from elsewhere) that regardless of their place in the order of the stases, causal arguments build on and set up other arguments. Like definitions and evaluations, they rarely appear in pure form, though we provide some examples of such pure causal arguments in the text. The situations that open the chapter suggest such ideal causal arguments, though they also rely on definitional issues.

We have found that students typically try to tackle causal arguments that reach too far for a regular class paper. Remember, too, that because the logic of causal arguments can be complex, students will likely benefit from extra time and help as they make causal claims. For useful models, you might turn to sports writing. Students can easily see how reasonable, informed observers can differ on why a team or an individual won or lost a competition.

Exercises

1. The causes of the following events and phenomena are quite well known and frequently discussed. But do you understand them well enough yourself to spell out the causes to someone else? Working in a group, see how well (and in how much detail) you can explain each of the following events or phenomena. Which explanations are relatively clear-cut, and which seem more open to debate?
    * tornadoes **[Clear-cut]**

35

If at all possible, have students view the Flash presentation on the Web so that they can see just how fully developed this argument is. In the class discussion or in the papers they write, push students to identify a potential audience for this presentation. How much prior knowledge does someone need to have about malaria to understand the argument? What kind of action does some one need to be able to take to be a target audience for this argument? Then ask them to focus on the argument itself: Would these claims be more effective if they were presented more simply? Do the bells and whistles of the presentation add to or detract from the main point? If they were to simplify this argument, what claims and evidence would they choose to emphasize?

- the Burning Man festival **[Open to debate]**
- the collapse of communism in Eastern Europe in 1989 **[Open to debate]**
- earthquakes **[Clear-cut]**
- the common cold **[Clear-cut]**
- the popularity of the *Harry Potter* films **[Open to debate]**
- the itching caused by a mosquito bite **[Clear-cut]**
- the economic recovery of 2004–2005 **[Open to debate]**
- a skid in your car on a slippery road **[Clear-cut]**
- the destruction of the Space Shuttle *Columbia* **[Open to debate]**
- the rise in cases of autism **[Open to debate]**

2–4. Exercises 2 and 3 would work well as large-group activities. For exercise 2, go around the class several times to see how far afield from the initial cause you can go. Alternatively, go around the class only once for each cause, but choose several initial causes to take to extremes. Exercise 4, which offers students practice at differentiating between types of causes, would also make a good in-class exercise, though you might have each student work individually or in pairs and then compare causal arguments.

●●● i·claim: VISUALIZING ARGUMENT (CD-ROM)
●●● TUTORIAL 06: ARGUMENTS HAVE LOGIC

Causal arguments are hard to make, in part because of the *post hoc, ergo propter hoc* fallacy. (Make sure students consult the glossary on the i*Claim CD-ROM to understand this term.) Tutorial 6, "Arguments Have Logic," will help them avoid this and other fallacies.

●●● i·cite: VISUALIZING SOURCES (CD-ROM)
●●● TUTORIAL 01: SOURCES ANSWER QUESTIONS

You might also have them go through Tutorial 1, "Sources Answer Questions," on the i*Cite CD. You could focus in particular on the discussion of the book *1491: New Revelations of the Americas before Columbus.* As a discipline, history is especially concerned with causal arguments, and Charles Mann articulates a causal argument about the population decline in the Americas. Have students pay special attention to how Mann talks about using sources to build his arguments. What sources can they consult to build their own causal arguments?

CHAPTER 11

Proposals

This chapter provides students with the opportunity to put all their previous work in the service of a complex argument. Proposal arguments have been popular in our classes because most students see them as the culmination of the semester's effort: once students have learned to analyze and produce arguments of definition, evaluation, and causation, proposal arguments make more sense. You can ask students to define terms carefully, to explain their evaluative criteria, or to explore the causal connections more thoroughly. This is a fun unit to teach because students put their rhetorical training to use and use language to change the world. If you review the stases before you teach the proposal argument, students will understand that the proposal does not exist in a vacuum but instead builds on what's come before.

Students often enjoy writing about practical problems on campus or in the community. Policy issues can make good papers, too, though you'll want to be careful that students don't tackle too much: it's easy for them to try to resolve world hunger in five pages. If your students write policy proposals, be sure to teach them the dangers of biting off more than they can chew.

We have asked students in our classes to do extensive audience analysis as part of the writing process. The chapter's guide to writing proposal arguments gives students some ideas about audience analysis, but you can go beyond what we provide. In the early stages of the writing process, ask students to write about their audience and consider the approaches that will be most rhetorically effective. Remind your students that if a proposal is to be accepted, it needs to be finely tuned to the demands of its audience. Toulmin logic could help some students understand their audience by drawing attention to warrants.

Not Just Words

These sample proposal arguments give students a great introduction to impressive multimedia presentations. No other student-written argument seems to lend itself to a variety of student presentations as well as the proposal argument. This exercise asks students to think particularly about a local audience, either their school or community. Such a focus allows students to identify their audience's interests more specifically, which usually leads to much better arguments. Many of your students are likely to have highly developed technical skills, so you might consider requiring them to create Web sites for their proposal arguments. But you might also ask them to think about what kinds of proposal arguments might benefit from simpler, less technical presentations.

Exercises

1. This exercise might be even more interesting if you ask your students to think of some possible defenses of off-the-wall suggestions. But perhaps the most important aspect of this exercise lies in pushing students to move beyond relatively simple solutions. For instance, some students might suggest "more education about the dangers of obesity" as a way of addressing the increasing rate of obesity in the United States. We have no objections to more education, but encourage your students to make more specific proposals. "More education" and "better funding" are relatively common proposal arguments that need to be explained fully and thoughtfully to be persuasive.

2–3. The exercises focus on two key issues for proposal arguments: developing claims that represent responses to real problems and tailoring proposals to a specific audience. Extend the exercises by asking students to examine a variety of proposals—from editorials in the student newspaper to large-scale governmental policy proposals—in terms of those same issues. How have the writers of policy proposals identified a real problem that's worth solving? How have editorial writers targeted their audience in their proposals? Also consider asking students to identify the proposals that might be hidden within other forms of argument: is the writer making a proposal without seeming to?

Because the "Arguments" section of the CD allows students to sort for "Proposals," you might ask students to look over several of the thumbnails that come up as proposal arguments. Is the claim primarily a policy or a practice proposal? What special strategies do these proposals use to appeal to a particular audience? Does the proposal call for a feasible action? You might discuss several of these proposals in class to help students formulate support for their own claims.

You might also ask them to review Tutorial 5, "Arguments Consider Multiple Viewpoints." Good proposal arguments must look forward to consider a wide variety of consequences, and consideration of multiple viewpoints helps students understand that audiences with conflicting goals can sometimes figure out a workable compromise.

CHAPTER 12

Style in Arguments

Figurative language is so prevalent—we argue in the chapter that it is "indispensable to language use"—that students will be able to find and analyze examples of figures from almost any source. One of our students once wrote a paper about figurative language in country music; she had a hard time finding lyrics that *weren't* highly figurative, and she argued that country music wouldn't be country music without figures.

This chapter might best be approached as part of another unit so you can show the relationship between figures and definition, for example. Metaphor is a definitional argument, after all. By combining this chapter with others, you can illustrate the ways figures argue and are not merely dressing on top of already established arguments. You can also push students to think carefully about what tropes they can include in their own arguments. Too often, students do not think much about their style, in part because they don't have the means to understand how to write stylishly. Use this chapter to help them become more conscious about *how* they write.

Challenge your students to find figures or tropes that we have not listed in this chapter. They could do research into the ancient rhetorical terms, or they could develop their own. Give students a piece of writing that is rich with figurative language, and ask them to identify each of the figures. Are there any sentences that seem to contain no schemes or tropes? Could it be that these sentences are figurative in ways students don't expect or recognize? Remind them that figures represent changes in the ordinary syntax or signification; how might these remaining sentences be read as different from the ordinary?

Exercises

1, 2, 4. These exercises ask students to become more conscious of style both as readers and as writers. These types of productive exercises are thousands of years old; students have been writing with schemes and tropes since at least the fifth century B.C. These kinds of exercises have persisted because they succeed — by helping students to recognize figurative language in others' sentences and to identify and use schemes and tropes more naturally in their own everyday writing.

3. In the following advertising slogans, identify the types of figurative language used: metaphor, simile, analogy, hyperbole, understatement, rhetorical question, antonomasia, irony, parallelism, antithesis, inverted word order, anaphora, or reversed structure.

- "Good to the last drop." (Maxwell House Coffee) **[Hyperbole]**
- "It's the real thing." (Coca-Cola) **[Antonomasia, understatement]**
- "Melts in your mouth, not in your hand." (M&M's) **[Parallelism]**
- "Be all that you can be." (U.S. Army) **[Reversed structure]**
- "Got Milk?" (America's Milk Processors) **[Rhetorical question]**
- "Breakfast of champions." (Wheaties) **[Hyperbole, antonomasia]**
- "Double your pleasure; double your fun." (Doublemint gum) **[Parallelism]**
- "Let your fingers do the walking." (the Yellow Pages) **[Metaphor]**

- "Think small." (Volkswagen) **[Understatement]**
- "Like a Rock." (Chevy Trailblazer) **[Simile]**
- "Real bonding, real popcorn, real butter, real good times." (Pop-Secret Popcorn) **[Anaphora]**

●●● i·claim: VISUALIZING ARGUMENT (CD-ROM)
●●● ARGUMENTS: SPEECHES

Ask your students to listen to the Jesse Jackson speech "The Rainbow Coalition" from the 1984 Democratic National Convention. Given that Jackson speaks deliberately and is frequently interrupted by applause, students will probably have time to identify some of the tropes and schemes that he employs. If the speech moves too quickly for them to follow or if you want to extend the exercise, ask students to find the full text online and analyze it for figurative language. You might also ask them to rewrite sections of the speech by omitting or changing the figures and to compare their creations to the original text. Be sure to allow time to discuss how these tropes enhance the spoken presentation, making the speech accessible as well as memorable.

CHAPTER 13

Humor in Arguments

This chapter lends itself better to short writing assignments than the chapters preceding it do. You *could* ask students to write four or five pages on some humorous topic (or to write a four- or five-page satire or parody), but the limited time usually available in writing classes means that you'll have to make some decisions about scope. More likely, you'll have a handful of students who want to use humor in at least one of their writing assignments, so this may be a chapter that those students study closely while others spend little time producing humorous arguments.

Still, humor often presents powerful arguments, and it's worthwhile to spend some time discussing how it works with the whole class. Some humor—like that in the animated television show *South Park*, for example—can be obviously argumentative, and many students will have little trouble identifying arguments from that show. Another animated TV program, *Family Guy*, is an example that most of your students will be familiar with, but its arguments might not be clear-cut to them. That show's humor is often more scattershot, but given some time students will be able to see how that show offers arguments. You might have students find examples of the writing of syndicated columnist Molly Ivins, *National Review Online* editor Jonah Goldberg, or ESPN.com Page 2 columnist Bill Simmons to see how authors can combine serious claims with humor. Once they see how these sources use humor, they should find it easier to see the arguments in some kinds of humor that they have been thinking of as argument-free. The concepts presented in this chapter—satire, parody, and detail—should help them improve their analyses.

Exercises

1. For each of the following items, list particular details that might contribute to a humorous look at the subject. **[Answers will vary.]**

> ## Not Just Words
>
> This project can be great fun for students, but it will take a bit of
> luck for them to stumble across a humorous visual argument.
> You might, therefore, encourage your students to manipulate
> the images to add some humor, which will test their application
> of the principles in this chapter. Alternatively, ask them to pro-
> vide captions that comment humorously on the image. In this
> case, you might have students bring in several images, display
> them in the classroom, and compete to write the wittiest caption.

- zealous environmentalists
- avaricious builders and developers
- aggressive drivers
- violent Hollywood films
- antiwar or hemp activists
- drivers of sport utility vehicles
- Martha Stewart
- high school coaches
- college instructors
- malls and the people who visit them

2–3. These exercises provide a few ideas for shorter writing assignments about humor, but they also require some effort on your students' part. If you want your class to explore humor without
spending days listening to friends or searching the Internet, you
could ask them to bring political cartoons to class for discussion.
Students could use Toulmin logic to analyze the many claims that
cartoons make; a single cartoon could make many claims, of
course. Ask your class to pay special attention to audience: Who
would find the cartoons funny? Who would not? Why?

●●● i•claim: VISUALIZING ARGUMENT (CD-ROM)
●●● TUTORIAL 03: ARGUMENTS HAVE GOALS

As we mention above, some students might have difficulty identifying
how some humor makes an argument. In those cases, the most common problem is that the students can't recognize the *goals* of the
humor. On the i*Claim CD, Tutorial 3, "Arguments Have Goals," includes an excerpt from Jonathan Swift's *A Modest Proposal*, which the

chapter also uses as an example. The CD allows students to read the excerpt and then click on six discussions of the goals of the essay. You might consider asking students who are writing a humorous piece to analyze some of their own text in this way; if they make their goals explicit, then they can make better choices about how to incorporate humor in their writing.

CHAPTER 14

Visual Arguments

As we suggested in earlier notes, most students are familiar with some techniques of visual argument even if they are not able to analyze those techniques critically. Images occupy such a large part of students' daily lives — in advertisements, on television, even in textbooks — that they are almost bombarded by visual arguments. But your students may need a framework for understanding such arguments so that they can review them critically in what they read and use them honestly in what they write.

This chapter offers that framework and takes a highly rhetorical approach to visual arguments. That is, the chapter does more than make recommendations about choosing fonts or effectively positioning items on a page (though it includes such advice as well); it also asks students to ponder the rhetorical impact of visual texts and images on readers.

The final sections of the chapter offer advice on reading and writing visual texts, as well as focus on rhetorical concepts. For instance, the elements of successful visual presentations are arranged according to three of the four appeals (or lines of argument) discussed earlier in the book so that writers are asked to consider visual arguments based on *character*, *logic*, and *emotions*. You might ask students to offer more examples of how these appeals translate when operating in highly visual texts such as advertisements or magazine covers. Indeed, magazine advertising is a rich source of visual arguments because almost all ads make the same claim: the reader should buy our product.

Once your class is comfortable analyzing advertisements, you could move on to other visual arguments, such as textbook illustrations, statistical charts and graphs, product logos, and photojournalism — all of which are visually represented in this chapter.

This exercise presents images that many students will find familiar, but they might never have thought about stamps as a kind of argument before. The discussion of these stamps should be a productive classroom exercise. If you would like to extend the exercise, you might have students consider other stamps that are available at <www.usps.com> (especially the year's commemorative stamps), or you might have them look at stamps from other decades, easily found online. How do arguments about America change from decade to decade? Or have them look at international stamps: how do the arguments made by stamps in other countries differ from those of American stamps?

Exercises

1–4. These exercises encourage students to write about visual images, a challenging task. Help your students develop a rich vocabulary of visual arguments by pointing them to the questions in the chapter under the heading "Analyzing Visual Elements of Arguments" and by doing several sample analyses in class. Once students are comfortable thinking critically about images in class, they will be more able to go off on their own to do critical analyses. You could bring to class examples of good writing about images: short pieces of art criticism, incisive movie reviews, columns by popular cultural critics.

●●● i·claim: VISUALIZING ARGUMENT (CD-ROM)
●●● ARGUMENTS: PACKAGING, POSTERS, AND COMICS

The i*Claim CD offers you and your students a common set of images to help apply the lessons of this chapter. Sort the "Arguments" for "Packaging, Posters, and Comics," and, if possible, display these images in the classroom so that students can analyze the visual arguments in groups. Alternatively, you might have the students write an analysis of one of the images from the CD as homework and then present their arguments to the rest of the class.

CHAPTER 15

Presenting Arguments

This chapter asks students to think about rhetoric as a set of tools that can help us shape our arguments in any number of different media. Help your students understand that audience awareness, style, and appeals to ethos, pathos, and logos are important means of persuasion in any argument.

Web sites present rich opportunities for rhetorical analysis: they usually contain textual and visual arguments; their organization can differ radically from print texts; and they face a potentially worldwide audience. But when students make their own arguments in electronic environments, the tools of rhetoric will guide their decisions.

This chapter also offers a rhetorical approach to spoken arguments. Writing courses are increasingly being called on to address speaking abilities, and persuasive, skillful oral presentation needs to be learned and practiced as surely as written presentation does. Even when you're not working on oral presentations, you might ask students to read aloud some of their work or sample arguments from other sources. Ask students to read carefully, perhaps even somewhat dramatically. They'll learn a great deal about how style helps create an argument, and you'll benefit from learning more about how they hear language.

Exercises

1-4. For exercise 1, make sure that students take no more than four paragraphs of a written essay to work with. You might suggest that they enlarge the type and increase the line spacing when they rewrite the text for oral argument. These changes will allow the student to highlight certain words and insert reminders to pause or slow down, ask for questions, or offer extratextual comments. Exercises 2, 3, and 4 ask students to examine other arguments and

Not Just Words

This exercise acknowledges that others usually decide how we should present our arguments. You might give students the option or even the requirement that they present one of their arguments for your class in a format other than a traditional essay. In particular, proposal arguments, which often come last in a writing class, lend themselves to a wide variety of formats. Asking students to consider alternative means of presentation almost always forces them to think more fully about the audience to whom they might address their arguments, a step that often results in higher-quality work.

figure out what makes them successful or unsuccessful. Have students bring their notes on these other arguments to class and work in small groups to discover what similarities or differences in strategies they identified. Were the strategies and their success determined by audience, personal preference, or something else?

●●● i•claim: VISUALIZING ARGUMENT (CD-ROM)
●●● TUTORIAL 02: ARGUMENTS HAVE CONTEXTS

On the i*Claim CD, have students review Tutorial 2, "Arguments Have Contexts." Ask them to pay special attention to the 15-second Adbusters spot, and discuss how effective the music and visuals are in that commercial. The "Assignments" section of the tutorial asks students to select an audience and context for their argument; you might also ask them to practice with an oral argument for these three audiences described. How would they deliver these arguments in different ways? Would they use different kinds of diction and figurative language?

CHAPTER 16

What Counts as Evidence

This can be a fun chapter for first-year writers, who, in our experience, believe that "real" evidence is always statistical or quantitative. When you show your students that they have a wide range of sources and forms available to them, their arguments will probably improve. As with some of the other chapters in Part 4, this chapter might be best taught in conjunction with a larger unit: combine a discussion of evidence with an assignment to write an evaluative argument, for instance.

Once you explain to your class that evidence can take many forms, you can move on to a discussion of the inventional role evidence can take: finding one piece of evidence can lead students not just to other pieces of evidence but also to new ways of making their arguments. Searching for evidence in libraries, interviews, or observations is not simply a one-way activity that goes from one source to the next. Instead, it can help students understand what claims they want to make, how they can approach the argument, and how they should tailor their arguments to an audience.

First-year writers have not usually chosen a major, but they might have some interest in a particular field or discipline. You could ask your students to interview faculty in their chosen field to find out what counts as evidence in that discipline. Students could then present their findings to the class. This is a two-part lesson: students have to *find* evidence *about* evidence.

Exercises

1–3. These exercises focus on the inventional role of evidence gathering, not just the technical questions of how to find evidence. It's important to discuss the limits of certain forms of evidence, as well as their strengths. Exercise 3, in which students observe another

Not Just Words

This exercise asks students to examine documents that have important consequences and to come to their own conclusions about what constitutes good evidence. Many of your students will not remember the incident surrounding these papers, and you might ask them to think about how their own political predilections influence their thoughts about the evidence. Are fans of George W. Bush less likely to demand visual proof that he shirked his National Guard duties? Do Bush critics expect those who doubt the veracity of these letters to present evidence for their opinion? This exercise offers an excellent opportunity for discussion of how our opinions and beliefs shape how we use and interpret evidence.

class, gives you an opportunity to talk about the limits of observations and field notes. You could develop other limit-setting exercises for other forms of evidence.

If you'd like to teach your students research techniques, you might think of scheduling a day in the library to walk around the reference areas and experiment with the catalog. Ask the librarians if they offer a guided tour or tutorial for students. Technical research skills are valuable, and first-year students rarely learn them except in their writing classes.

●●● i•cite: VISUALIZING SOURCES (CD-ROM)
●●● TUTORIAL 04: SOURCES HELP YOU SHAPE WHAT YOU THINK

You might ask students to consult the i*Cite CD for Tutorial 4, "Sources Help You Shape What You Think." Ask your students to pay particular attention to the first section, which traces how *The Smoking Gun* investigated James Frey's memoir, *A Million Little Pieces*. Does the testimony of Frey's high school classmate have much weight? What about the evidence of Frey's high school yearbook photo? Can we accept that photo as a representative picture from Frey's adolescence? Is the testimony by the police officers more reliable? In short, use this tutorial to help press students to think critically and skeptically about evidence—and to help them figure out how to build an argument from pieces of evidence that might be insufficient on their own or seem otherwise disconnected.

CHAPTER 17

Fallacies of Argument

Our experience has been that first-year writers can really do well in a unit on fallacies. They enjoy finding the fallacies in newspaper editorials, Web pages, and even their own papers (it's a little embarrassing to have fallacious reasoning pointed out, but students usually appreciate the help). And searching for fallacies can be like a treasure hunt: you know you're going to find something somewhere, but you don't know what or where.

The fallacies we've listed here constitute only a few of the many that logicians and rhetoricians have identified through the years. You could ask your students to do research into the topic of fallacies. If you combine this chapter with the one on evidence, you could also make this a disciplines-based activity because fallacies differ from field to field.

It's important to note that fallacies are not always mortal errors in argument but that they represent reasoning that is in *some way* faulty or that is likely to be rejected by a *particular* audience. Arguments that one audience might accept could be rejected by another audience that considers the reasoning fallacious. We've given some examples of this problem in the text, but you could find many more in the pages of your local newspaper or even in your students' papers.

Exercises

1. Following is a list of political slogans or phrases that may be examples of logical fallacies. Discuss each item to determine what you may know about the slogan; then decide which, if any, fallacy might be used to describe it.
   - "Leave no child behind." (George Bush policy and slogan) **[Sentimental appeal]**
   - "It's the economy, stupid." (sign on the wall at Bill Clinton's campaign headquarters) **[Bandwagon appeal; possibly faulty causality]**

This particular exercise is likely to provoke a spirited response from students, most of whom have seen years and years of warnings against drugs and alcohol. To extend the exercise, ask students to examine the archives at <www.adcouncil.org> and choose what they think are the most effective public service advertisements. You might also ask them to create their own posters or presentations that they think would be more effective than what they've seen in the past.

- "Nixon's the one." **[Begging the question; equivocation]**
- "Remember the Alamo." **[Possibly a *non sequitur* or faulty causality]**
- "Make love, not war." (antiwar slogan during the Vietnam War) **[Either/or; dogmatism]**
- "A chicken in every pot" **[Possibly a *non sequitur* or faulty causality]**
- "No taxation without representation" **[Possibly a *non sequitur*]**
- "There's no free lunch." **[Possibly dogmatism]**
- "Loose lips sink ships." **[Possibly a *non sequitur* or faulty causality]**
- "Guns don't kill, people do." (NRA slogan) **[Faulty causality]**
- "If you can't stand the heat, get out of the kitchen." **[Either/or]**

2–5. Your students might really enjoy exercise 2 if you encourage them to write extreme examples of the fallacies. It's a little like asking them to engage in a liars' contest, and students might enjoy reading their results aloud. Exercises 3 and 4 ask students to find fallacies in other texts. These exercises might prove to be difficult, but that difficulty will help students understand that many so-called fallacies are audience-specific. Exercise 5, which asks students to see how other writers read fallacies, might also reinforce the slipperiness of calling an argument fallacious.

Under the "Arguments" section on the CD, ask students to sort for "Fallacies." The CD presents nine samples, and you can ask students to identify the fallacies present in each argument; there will probably be some interesting variation in labeling the fallacies. You might ask the students then to try to make the same argument without depending on the fallacy: Is that even possible with all of these arguments? Is it ever OK to offer a consciously fallacious argument?

CHAPTER 18

Intellectual Property, Academic Integrity, and Avoiding Plagiarism

First-year writers have probably received some instruction in the problems of intellectual property. They likely have heard of plagiarism in high school, have been taught not to copy others' work, and understand that plagiarizing is a form of cheating. But plagiarism is only a small part of the intellectual property debate, and its parameters are far from well defined. You can help your students learn to use sources responsibly if you show them the range of activities that could reasonably constitute plagiarism, from simple copying of text without quotation or attribution to including images on a Web site that the student did not create. Students need to learn that intellectual property can be as jealously guarded as material property, if not more so: material goods can usually be replaced, but intellectual work is not easy to return.

The first-year writing class is usually the place where students learn to respect intellectual property rights and where they struggle with the boundaries of appropriate attribution. As the teacher, you can decide how strict to be with violations of intellectual property. Our experience has been that for the most part, students do not intend to cheat or to copy without attribution. In most cases, they have simply misunderstood the rules of attribution or have not thought carefully enough about their use of sources. If you use a process model in your course, you could encourage these students to write another draft, this time with appropriate use of sources. Not all incidents of plagiarism are simply well-intentioned mistakes, but we argue for a generous conception of teaching in the first-year course. If students continue to violate the boundaries of intellectual property after you've been thorough in your instruction, you should take appropriate action.

Not Just Words

Intellectual property can be a hot-button issue with many students because of the lawsuits brought against people who have downloaded music and video from the Web, but this essential chapter may not be the most exciting reading for students. Fortunately, this is an entertaining exercise that asks students to produce their own parody. Ask students to review Chapter 13, "Humor in Arguments," before they create their parody.

Exercises

1–4. The exercises for this chapter focus mainly on the differences among the various forms of intellectual-property protection. You could combine these exercises with a discussion of the protections available to people in different academic fields. For example, how do scientists in college biology departments protect their work? What about historians? How does each person build on previous work in the field without "copying"? Exercise 4 should be particularly useful for illustrating that intellectual property is as important an issue outside the classroom as it is inside it.

●●● i•cite: VISUALIZING SOURCES (CD-ROM)
●●● SOURCE PRACTICE

The i*Cite CD's "Source Practice" section allows you to assign a useful practice that will help students make sense of this chapter. Have students practice incorporating sources when you talk about intellectual property. As we mention above, many cases of student plagiarism come from a misunderstanding of how to cite sources properly, so having extra practice citing sources can be helpful for students. Don't be shy about holding them to high standards with citation: the first-year writing course may be the only class that ever teaches students how to use sources properly.

CHAPTER 19

Evaluating and Using Sources

Many of our comments from Chapter 18 apply here, too: students rarely *try* to cheat or get away with misusing intellectual property. You will serve your students—and the purposes of the first-year writing course — if you consider most problems with attribution to be mistakes rather than cheating attempts: students simply don't understand the parameters of responsible use. Many students have to struggle to write their own thoughts and arguments; integrating others' ideas is a real challenge.

Assessing sources can also be a challenge for students. Because the Internet makes finding material so easy, some students will be satisfied with the thousands of hits they get on any search. You will have to teach your students to be very critical of Internet sources: for example, a personal homepage on legalizing marijuana is significantly less credible than refereed research on hemp agriculture, but your students might not see the difference. The chapter includes a list of questions students can ask to determine the quality of any source, electronic or not.

Not Just Words

Students are frequently skeptical of media sources, and this exercise might help them think carefully about the many layers involved in a media presentation. A discussion of who is responsible for this photo caption mistake and whether the newspaper's later correction is adequate might lead to some disagreement among students. Press them to articulate what makes a source reliable: What level of accuracy should we be able to expect from journalists? What kinds of mistakes are forgivable? What kind of correction can excuse an error?

Exercises

1–4. The exercises focus largely on the problems of authority and credibility in assessing sources. You could ask students to compile a "first-pass" bibliography on a given topic and then to make a second pass, evaluating the sources for inclusion in a shorter list.

The chapter describes the differences among quotations, paraphrases, and summaries, but the exercises do not address these differences. Students will probably benefit from practicing these techniques, though the more context you can give them, the better. Rather than ask for summaries or paraphrases that are unrelated to students' long writing assignments, suggest that students write paraphrases or summaries in preparation for their other work. Carefully integrate the techniques into the larger concerns of the course. Electronic sources create special bibliographic difficulties, too: it's easy to surf through the Internet without taking thorough notes about where you've been and when you were there.

●●● **i•cite:** VISUALIZING SOURCES (CD-ROM)
●●● SOURCE PRACTICE

The i*Cite CD contains a "Source Practice" section that will be a valuable complement to this chapter. You might have students begin the practice with the Web sites: students seem to have special trouble with evaluating Web sites, even though they use the Web as their research tool of choice. However, they'll need the experience evaluating different types of sources, so when working on this chapter, have the students practice evaluating at least four sources — one of each kind available on the CD (books, Web sites, articles, and audio/visual).

CHAPTER 20

Documenting Sources

Most of this chapter is concerned with the technical details of the MLA and APA citation systems, not with the way citation and documentation constitute a form of argument. The details are not hard to master, but they are complicated and reward careful attention. Our experience has been that first-year students will make up their own citation systems—with some mix of dates, names, and titles, rarely consistent—unless they are asked to follow MLA or APA guidelines carefully.

Not Just Words

This exercise calls attention to the appearance of citations and how Web sites have chosen a form of documentation that helps to emphasize readability, as the links do not distract much from the text. If you're teaching MLA format, you might talk about how the MLA style attempts to minimize distractions to the reader—by encouraging researchers to include authors' names in the text of the paper rather than just in the parenthetical citation and by placing most parenthetical citations at the ends of sentences. Part of the goal of teaching citation, perhaps, is teaching students that a documentation style is not just a random collection of rules but a system designed to make intellectual inquiry open and honest.

Exercises

1. This exercise asks students to identify the ways certain citation systems make arguments in themselves. Draw your students' attention to the relative placements of author, date of publication,

and title in MLA and APA styles. You could ask your students to develop alternate citation styles that reflect some other values or priorities: How would they cite sources if they were concerned primarily with the author's credibility? Would book sales ever be an appropriate measure to cite in a bibliography?

2. This exercise allows students to practice citing works (e.g., songs) that they might be surprised to learn are covered by MLA and APA. This exercise should be fairly quick and simple for students, but make sure that they take the time to get their citations correct. Students must pay close attention to details to make sure they cite correctly.

●●● **i·cite:** VISUALIZING SOURCES (CD-ROM)
●●● SOURCE PRACTICE

As with the two previous chapters, the "Source Practice" section on the i*Cite CD will be an invaluable aid for helping students make sense of documentation. For this chapter, you might ask students to practice citing sources, once again emphasizing the Web sites section. Because Web sites do not have a standard format yet, students need extra help figuring out how to find the information they need to cite in addition to the correct format for their citation. Though these kinds of exercises take some time, students usually need and benefit from the extra practice.

CHAPTER 21

Who's the Fairest of Them All?

The readings in this chapter examine representations of the human body. In doing so, they raise complex questions about the extent to which the media are descriptive or normative. If they are descriptive, they reflect society. If they are normative, they evaluate and judge society—either openly or indirectly, by setting standards against which real people and events come to be judged. Thus, these readings lead to questions such as the following:

- Do the media reflect society as it is? Should they?
- Do the images of people we see in the media become yard-sticks against which we judge ourselves or against which others judge us? If so, to what extent are these portrayals and judgments harmful? Why?
- Are the media both descriptive and normative? To what extent and in which cases?

P. Byrnes *It Begins* p. 588

1. Is the baby in this cartoon male or female? Why do you think so?

   Answers will vary, but the baby is likely to be considered female because women are traditionally considered to be more interested in their looks than men are.

2. What is the "it" of "It begins"?

   The word "it" refers to self-deprecation based on appearance or to preoccupation with appearance.

3. Why is this cartoon humorous? What knowledge about American culture does it assume?

   It is humorous because we know that babies don't really think about the size of their posteriors. The cartoon assumes knowledge about Americans' preoccupation with ap-

pearance and also about the harmfulness of an excessive preoccupation with body image.

Classroom Exercise: focus on the argument

You have undoubtedly heard that physical appearance is increasingly important in the United States and elsewhere. Do you agree with this observation? Using only *your own* personal experiences as evidence — not what you've read or what your friends or relatives have related to you — support or refute the claim that appearance has, in your lifetime, become more important as a measure of a person's worth. (We imagine that many students will find it difficult to avoid citing what they've read or heard from others. This exercise is intended to make students aware of the extent to which their beliefs are shaped by the experiences of others and also to enhance their ability to assess different types of evidence.)

Ellen Goodman *The Culture of Thin Bites Fiji* pp. 589–591

1. What is Goodman's argument?

She argues that popular culture teaches girls and women to hate and harm themselves.

How does she build it around Becker's study while not limiting herself to that evidence alone?

She does it by framing Becker's study within her own prose. She opens with an invitation to her readers to imagine a situation that sets up the background for describing Becker's research. She concludes by pulling back and adding her own commentary and recontextualizing the discussion in terms of the Columbine school killings.

2. What cultural knowledge does Goodman assume her *Boston Globe* audience to have?

She expects them to have familiarity with popular TV shows, knowledge of the high incidence of eating disorders among young women, and awareness of incidents of killings in schools by young male students.

How does she use allusions to American TV programs to build her argument? Note, for example, that she sometimes uses such allusions as conversational asides — "All that and these islanders didn't even get *Ally McBeal*," and "At this rate, we owe the islanders at least one year of the ample lawyer Camryn Manheim in *The Practice* for free" — to establish her ethos.

Answers will vary. One strong possibility is that Goodman invokes shared knowledge to establish credibility with her audience and develop ethos.

In what other ways do allusions to TV programs contribute to Goodman's argument?

They provide specific evidence of the material viewed by Fijians.

3. At least by implication, if not in fact, Goodman makes a causal argument about the entertainment industry, women's body image, and the consequences of such an image. What sort of causal argument does she set up? (For a discussion of causal arguments, see Chapter 10.)

She uses Anne Becker's research about teens in Fiji to argue about the effects of the entertainment industry on women's body image: teenage girls who watch popular American television shows develop a skewed image of the ideal female body size and shape.

How effective do you find it? Why?

Answers will vary.

4. Writing assignment

Classroom Exercise: focus on the world

Goodman's conclusion links eating disorders and recent school killings, stating that the media heavily influence adolescents to be destructive. How persuasive is this link? How similar are the two types of destructive behavior that Goodman cites — the destruction of others committed by certain boys and the self-destruction committed by certain girls? How is the role of the media similar in the two types of destruction? How is it different?

Anne E. Becker *Abstract, Discussion,* and *Conclusion* of
*Television, Disordered Eating, and
Young Women in Fiji: Negotiating
Body Image and Identity During
Rapid Social Change*   pp. 592–600

1. How does Becker link exposure to Western media to the changing
   notions young Fijian women have of their own bodies?

   **The author interviewed young women in a rural town of
   Fiji three years after the introduction of television to the
   community. The social interviews focused on body image,
   and the researcher also analyzed the girls' references to
   media images.**

   Why, specifically, does Becker claim these women now want to be
   thin? How are these changes linked to other social changes occurring in Fiji, to adolescence, and to gender, especially in small-scale
   societies?

   **Young women's focus has shifted from their communities'
   traditional values to the Western value of consumerism.
   They identify with television characters and celebrity
   lifestyles, and they equate too much weight with laziness
   and thinness with success. Fiji is also facing economic and
   social changes as it looks out onto a globalizing world.
   Young women are especially susceptible to these outside
   media forces in a climate of rapid social change when they
   are searching for role models. Women in general must consider self-presentation for social status in an environment
   where merit is ascribed, not achieved.**

2. As Becker notes, she relies on qualitative data—specifically interview data—to support her arguments. Why are such data especially appropriate, given her goals of understanding the changing
   social meanings of body image for young Fijian women as part of
   other rapid social changes taking place? (For a discussion of firsthand evidence, see Chapter 16.)

   **Interview data are firsthand evidence that may not be avail-
   able through observations or even questionnaires. The perspective of a person involved in a specific situation is
   invaluable, especially in a changing social atmosphere
   where other types of evidence may be difficult to collect.**

3. Throughout the Discussion and Conclusion sections, Becker repeatedly qualifies her arguments to discourage readers from extending them further than she believes her data warrant. Find two cases where she does so, and explain in what specific ways she reminds readers of the limits of her claims. (For a discussion on qualifying claims and arguments, see Chapter 6.)

Answers will vary, but some examples include her use of "minimally" and "quite possibly." When Becker tells us that "Minimally . . . narrative data reflect a shift in fashion," she lets the reader know that her data reports at least this fact and might have further implications. Her use of a qualifier in "Quite possibly . . . disordered eating may also be a symbolic embodiment of the anxiety and conflict the youth experience" suggests that the eating behavior of women is more complicated than a reaction to seeing beautiful people on television.

4. These excerpts from Becker's article obviously represent research writing for an academic audience. What functions does each of the reprinted sections serve for the article's readers, and why is each located where it is? Why, for example, is an abstract placed at the beginning of an article? Why are keywords a valuable part of this abstract?

The delineated sections of the article give structure to the paper and create focal points for different information about the study. The abstract tells us what to expect from the paper as a whole, so it comes first. The discussion analyzes the data that have been presented. The conclusion draws the various points together with some implications for further research or action. The keywords present the main themes of the paper so that the reader can judge the relevance of the article to the information that they seek.

5. Writing assignment

Classroom Exercise: focus on the argument

Becker reports that beauty standards are changing in Fiji due to the influx of Western ideals, specifically television images of slender women. Consider your response to this research. Would you have imagined that television could have such an effect in a culture with a long history of appreciating full-figure women? Is it a problem that women want to be thin, or is just their dangerous manner of losing weight at issue? Should one or both issues be addressed? Should young Fijian women be encouraged to return to their traditional beauty ideals? Using Becker's article as your source material, hold a debate or round table discussion in your class.

Jane Stern *Big,* Review of *Fat Girl: A True Story*
by Judith Moore   pp. 601–604

1. What functions might you expect a book review like Stern's to serve? How are reviews arguments?

   A review creates an argument about the relative merits of a particular book, artwork, or business. A piece of this sort lets readers know what to expect from whatever is being reviewed and places the work in a social context.

   What sorts of evaluative criteria does Stern use in reviewing Moore's book? How appropriate are they? Do the visual elements contribute to the review? Why or why not?

   Stern evaluates Moore's book in several ways. She notes that the author breaks away from the common theme of losing weight and complaining about weight and instead explores how she became fat and how it has made her who she is. In her closing, Stern notes that the book's editing and jacket design were not what she would expect for such a good author.

2. How effectively does Stern use quotations from Moore's book? How would quotations, especially in a book review, both tell and show something about the book being reviewed?

   Answers will vary, but the quotations about dieting, unhappy family life, and food excess suggest that much of the book will discuss the interaction of these three themes.

   Choose two quotations, and explain how Stern uses them as a part of her evaluative judgment.

   Answers will vary.

3. How does Stern characterize Moore's ethos? How does Stern create her own ethos as a writer and reviewer? How would you characterize her ethos?

Stern's use of a quotation about Moore's attitude toward her subject matter presents the style of writing and narrative ethos that a reader of the book can expect. By positively evaluating the book author's style, by making favorable references to the author as a "veteran" of diets or the creator of a "rallying cry," and by suggesting that she also has been fat since childhood, Stern reveals her own exasperation with both "fat haters" and "do-gooders."

4. Writing assignment

Classroom Exercise: focus on the world

Both Stern and Moore talk frankly about being fat. How comfortable are you with this tone and point of view? Do you think that Americans focus too much on body appearance? Should we be concerned about weight to a certain degree, or does personal acceptance mean not trying to change at all? Do you agree that some people naturally have a much larger body type than is considered attractive in the media?

W. Charisse Goodman *One Picture Is Worth a Thousand Diets* pp. 605–611

1. Goodman contends that "[m]ovies, television, magazines, newspapers, and preachifying self-help books all reinforce and amplify the ignorant stereotypes about fat people that America holds so close and dear; taken together, they constitute a framework of 'petrified opinions' which few dare to question" (paragraph 1). What sorts of evidence does she use to support this claim? How is Goodman's evidence similar to and different from the evidence used by Jane Stern in her review of Judith Moore's *Fat Girl*?

   Goodman focuses on firsthand observation evidence taken from various forms of media, creating a survey of the images that we see daily, while Stern uses secondhand evidence that she collected by reading Moore's memoir and then comments on her reactions to the memoir. Goldberg focuses more on specific examples and Goodman more on compiled examples and trends, but both talk about advertising and the acceptability of antifat humor in U.S. society.

2. Examine how Goodman uses quotations as evidence, especially the opening quote about "petrified opinions" from Mark Twain and the one from the personals section of a newspaper ("Be any race, be yourself, but be beautiful") in paragraphs 15 and 23. In what ways do quotations help structure the argument?

They provide a recurring theme for stylistic purposes, and they provide framing devices for the conclusion.

3. Personal ads are especially interesting as arguments because of their brevity. Examine some personal ads in a local newspaper, surveying systematically the images that emerge of the ideal male or female partner. What images express the ideals for each group?

Answers will vary.

To what extent are these ideals the ones that occur most frequently in television, movies, and magazines?

To a large extent

Are you concerned about the gap between the ideal and the reality of everyday life? Why or why not?

Answers will vary.

4. Writing assignment

Classroom Exercise: focus on the world

(Note: This exercise would work well alone or as preparation for the writing assignment in Exercise 4. Bring in, or have students bring in, copies of recent popular magazines.) Working in groups, compile data and analyze the images of people portrayed. Before you start, make a list of the categories you'll be looking for—women/men; advertisements/articles; size; positive/negative characteristics; and so on. In addition, consider whether the person depicted is intended for the viewer *to identify with* or *to consider as an other* (for example, a photo of a woman romping in the surf is meant for viewers to identify with, whereas a snarling "cafeteria lady" is certainly meant to represent some "other"). Once you have a composite picture of all the visual images in the magazine, analyze the underlying message that each magazine makes about body size.

New York Times *Reshaping America: Popular Cosmetic Procedures, by Sex* pp. 612–613

1. How might this graphic have been used to support the argument made by the title of the article it accompanied, "Plastic Surgery Gets a New Look?" (In fact, this graphic appeared not on the first page of the article but on the page where the article was continued and carried the title "Plastic Surgery: Drastic Is Out. Subtle Is In.")

   This graphic presents the percentage change in different cosmetic procedures from 1997 to 2003 with statistics that show that nose reshaping and eyelid surgery have increased some, while fat injections, breast augmentation, and liposuction for women have more than doubled. Botox injection for women has increased 300 times, and for men it has increased by almost 600.

2. One might say that this graphic has three parts. What are they, and how does each contribute to the graphic as a whole?

   The data represent current trends in cosmetic procedures from women and men. The percentages show changes in the numbers of each procedure between 1997 and 2003. The dollar amounts show the cost of each procedure as of 2003.

3. Are you surprised by the information presented in this graphic? Why or why not?

   Answers will vary.

   How is the visual presentation here for women and men especially effective in conveying a great deal of information clearly? The focus of the visual information in this graphic is the number of procedures for women and men. What would we see if the information for "Percentage change since 1997" were presented as bar charts? Compare, for example, the increase in Botox and eyelid surgery for women and men since 1997.

   The circles represent the 2003 relative popularity of certain procedures, while the percentage change, listed below each graphic, highlights how much more or less popular the procedure became between 1997 and 2003. Moving the procedure prices to a side bar decreased the amount of information written on the main table, providing clarity.

4. Writing assignment

Classroom Exercise: focus on the world

Do you find it surprising that men are embracing plastic surgery? What pressures might be pushing this phenomenon? What examples can you think of in the media that might cause men to question their own appearances? Should we consider it a positive trend or at least a matter of personal taste to have elective surgeries? What about people who feel that a particularly unattractive body part is holding them back financially or socially or is causing them distress? Under what circumstances would you consider plastic surgery yourself? (These questions may serve as discussion starters in class, as the basis for an opinion piece written and shared in class, or as issues for a team debate.)

Rob Walker *Social Lubricant: How A Marketing*
Campaign Became the Catalyst for
a Societal Debate   pp. 614–617

1. Whatever else Walker is doing, he is making an argument about advertising, body image, and public debate. How would you characterize this argument? What kind of argument is it? (For a discussion of four kinds of arguments, see Chapter 1.) What evidence can you cite for your claim? Once you have decided what kind of argument Walker is making, evaluate how well he makes it, making explicit your criteria for evaluation.

   Walker's argument is one of quality: is this a positive change in advertising? He points out the paradox of finding real models to validate everyday beauty while at the same time using them as a vehicle to sell thigh-firming cream. Throughout the article, Walker points out the duplicitous nature of the campaign.

2. While the Dove survey of women showed that they responded well to efforts to challenge the "only-thin-is-beautiful" stereotype common in American society, it didn't investigate why they might feel this way. Walker seeks to do so in this essay (paragraphs 4–5). How well does he make his case? In other words, do you agree or disagree with his analysis of American women's motivations for rejecting the idea that a woman must be thin to be beautiful? Why or why not? Can you think of reasons he might have included but did not?

Answers will vary, but Walker points out in his analysis that marketing campaigns have been a major proponent of thin images and that an antiperfection message from marketers is heartening. It is also possible that women may be weary of both the self-improvement movement and thinness expectation.

3. What sort of argument does the visual that accompanied Walker's text make? How does it add to or detract from his argument?

   The tongue-in-cheek visual argues that linking Dove body cream to essential beauty is ridiculous. A beauty enhancer is out of place in such a context, just as it should be considered ridiculous in the lives of real women.

   How does appreciating its argument depend crucially on the reader's familiarity with Sandro Botticelli's painting from about 1485, *The Birth of Venus*, reproduced here? Can you give examples of other visual allusions — images whose full interpretation depends on knowledge of other images to which they make reference?

   To appreciate the juxtaposition of the beauty aid and Venus, one must understand that Venus is the Roman goddess of love and beauty.

4. Writing assignment

Classroom Exercise: focus on the world

One might argue that the Dove ads are selling much more than firming cream. What else do these ads sell or promote? Think of other well-known ad campaigns (such as Levi, Old Navy, and Abercrombie & Fitch). Aside from the product itself, what else were these ad campaigns promoting? What do companies have to gain by promoting other images of lifestyles or gender roles in their campaigns?

Meghan Daum *Those Unnerving Ads Using "Real" Women*   pp. 618–621

1. What's Daum's argument? In other words, why does she find the "Real Women" ads disconcerting? What, according to her, is the real reason that all of us want to see "preternatural" (paragraph 9)

people as models rather than people who look like us? Do you agree or disagree? Why or why not?

In addition to noting that the Dove ad campaign is selling firming cream by adopting feminist rhetoric, Daum argues that Americans want to distance ourselves from the reality of the body with all of its hair and "jiggle." By using professionally beautiful people in advertising, we can avoid confronting our bodies and identify with the ideal. While we might love ourselves, we do not want to expose our imperfections to the world.

2. What does Daum mean when she contends that actual intimacy is "raw" (paragraph 12)? How does her word choice in this case make her argument memorable? How does she support her claim that intimacy is raw? Why is this claim crucial to her argument?

Actually intimacy comes with all the insecurity of making oneself vulnerable. This use of "raw" is memorable for the strength it has as a pejorative adjective. Daum supports her argument with the example of a bedroom, which represents comfort and intimacy but also implies a protection from peering eyes.

3. In what ways is there "Machiavellian irony" in using "vaguely feminist rhetoric to sell cellulite cream" (paragraph 7)? Where's the irony? Why might Daum label it "Machiavellian"? How does this allusion to Machiavelli represent an argument?

Machiavelli was a proponent of manipulation as a means to an end. In this case, selling firming cream overrides any conflict of interest in celebrating the simple and internal beauties of women in a Web page. By calling Dove's sales technique Machiavellian, Daum is pointing out the duplicitous nature of the company's message.

4. Writing assignment

Classroom Exercise: focus on the argument

Do you agree with Daum's argument that we prefer to see beautiful people in the media because we are put off by the "rawness" of the reality of our bodies? If so, do you imagine that these feelings exist across cultures? What aspects of American culture have made people distance themselves from wanting to see both themselves in firming-cream ads and also things like body hair and other body functions?

Guy Trebay *When Did Skivvies Get Rated NC-17?*   pp. 622–628

1. Although the tone of this piece is often light and even humorous in spots, Trebay makes some very strong claims about changes in American culture's attitudes toward the male body over the past few decades. Among these claims would be statements like the following: "In the decades since the first Calvin Klein ads, men have been substantially feminized and also have genially adapted to their transformation into objects of an erotic gaze." (paragraph 9)

"[Guys] care less, apparently, about assumptions regarding their sexual orientation than being able to fill out a pair of low-slung jeans from companies like Diesel and G-Star." (paragraph 23) Do you agree with such claims? Why or why not?

Answers will vary.

Do you believe that young men face the sorts of pressures with respect to their bodies as "objects of erotic gaze" that young women have faced for generations? Why or why not?

Answers will vary.

2. What does the author mean by the phrase "the democratization of desire" (paragraph 11)? How, in American culture, is such a phrase an argument of sorts? How does the alliteration—the repetition of the initial consonant sound, *d* in this case—contribute to his argument?

In America, democracy is seen as an essential part of freedom. In that sense, democratization of anything is a liberation. Here the author means that now men have the opportunity to be objects of desire, just like women. The alliteration of the *d* strengthens the argument through its poetic structure.

Is the democratization of desire a good thing? Why or why not?

Answers will vary.

3. In light of Trebay's argument, which many people would accept, that the shift in attitudes toward the male body has been encouraged by a certain segment of the gay male population, what sort of argument is the brand name Adam + Eve? To whom might you expect such a name to appeal? To whom might it not appeal? Why?

The brand name Adam + Eve connotes a heterosexual couple — the story of the creation of the first man and woman as told in the book of Genesis in the Hebrew scriptures. This brand name would then argue for a heteronormative focus of erotic desire on the male body. This product would then appeal to straight men and women, but it could possibly have a crossover effect in the gay community.

4. Trebay contends that just a few years ago, the sorts of images one finds on today's men's underwear boxes would have been found only in sex shops. He also notes that the percentage of such men's underwear sales is much smaller than the percentage going to "white cotton basics." Given these two observations, why, in your opinion, are department stores full of displays featuring such underwear and advertising?

It is possible that those who shop in department stores are likely to buy such underwear but do not represent a majority of the general underwear-buying public.

5. Writing assignment

Classroom Exercise: focus on the argument

When did men start to become "objects of erotic gaze"? Is the "democratization of desire" a step forward in the development of an egalitarian society? Is this development the natural result of challenges to gender roles? Has society changed, or has the way we talk about such things changed (haven't women long joked about cabana boys?)? If advertising has reached this point of sexualization and explicitness, what comes next? Write an argument about the future in which you describe what men's underwear advertising will look like in another ten to twenty years, and share your ideas in class.

Making a Visual Argument: Three Views on Body Image

Toby Old, From *Waterlog: The Beach Series*

Mikhaela Blake Reid *Your Yucky Body: A Repair Manual*

Jason Stirman, *Reflections: Body Image Seminar*
Crossroads Baptist
Church   pp. 629–632

1. The people in the photograph by Toby Old are, indeed, "real people," actual people who happened to be at Orchard Beach on the day in 2002 when the photograph was taken. How might we read the photograph as an argument about body image? How would the photo be different if the woman on the right were not holding two Barbie dolls by their hair in her left hand?

   The juxtaposition of the women and the Barbie dolls in Old's photo argues for an overturning or flouting of the rules of body beauty. Without the dolls, it would be more difficult to get that reading from two women in bathing suits.

2. These selections range from the purely visual (Old's photograph) to the text dominant (Reid's cartoon) with two of the selections including at least some text. What roles does the text play in each of these three selections? How do the text and the visual image work together to create the argument? How would the arguments be different if there were not text? If there were no image?

   Reid uses text to create humor as she describes or annotates her drawings. Stirman's flyer for the Baptist Church uses text to make its point about the fiction of a Barbie doll body. Without the text, Reid's cartoon would be opaque at best, and Stirman's Barbie flyer would be indistinguishable from an advertisement for the doll. Without the visual, the same arguments could be made, but they would not be as interesting.

3. How do the selections by Reid and the found flyer use humor to make their point? Are the two equally effective? What are the strengths of each? (Why, by the way, might a church be sponsoring a seminar on body image? Who might be the audience for such a seminar?)

The two arguments use humor to highlight the impossibility of the standards of beauty that they describe. Reid uses the grotesque humor of perfection taken too far, while Stirman's flyer invites us to conjure up the image of a crawling Barbie figure. The church may be sponsoring an interesting event to draw more young people to the congregation, or it may be aiming at its own young people or adults.

4. Writing assignment

Classroom Exercise: focus on the world

All of the visuals in this selection argue against the stereotypes of the perfection of beauty. While many people are quick to agree and support such arguments, most (including many of those who argue for natural beauty) go to great lengths to improve their image with makeup, hair products and dye, teeth whitener, jewelry, and more. Where are the boundaries between taking care of oneself, making a good impression, improving upon nature, and taking excessive measures? Should more distinctions be made? Less? How might these distinctions vary by culture or even by gender? (These questions can serve to start a class discussion or a reaction paper, or students may choose to defend a specific level of beauty aspiration.)

Wrap-up Exercises for Constructing Arguments about Beauty and the Media

Here are several writing assignments that deal with the chapter as a whole. They are suitable for extended projects. In addition, item 3 would make an excellent in-class essay question.

1. Building on the assignment in which you analyzed advertisements for men's underwear, repeat the assignment by examining advertisements for women's underwear or cologne. When you have finished, write an essay in which you compare the ways in which men's and women's bodies have been used in advertisements for selling underwear or cologne. The essay may be primarily descriptive (enumerating your findings) or persuasive (using your results to evaluate the differences in the ways women's and men's bodies have been used in selling underwear or cologne).

2. Goodman's article on the images of heavy women in the media considered personal ads as a form of argument. Another popular form of argument is the bumper sticker. Collect an assortment of bumper stickers—perhaps a dozen or two—about a single issue (or about opposite sides of a single issue), and write an essay in which you examine the bumper stickers as arguments. In all cases, the argument made by the bumper sticker will likely be enthymematic. Hence, you'll need to consider the logic of the argument and any premises that are not stated but are assumed by the bumper sticker's creators. You may decide to make your essay descriptive, reporting on how argument in bumper stickers works, or you may decide to make it persuasive. Possible topics and approaches include analyzing how bumper-sticker arguments about a particular issue characterize the potential stances one can take on that issue, evaluating the fairness or efficacy of such argumentation, and speculating on the reasons that bumper-sticker arguments are popular in the United States. For each of these argumentative topics, you should build your case around specific bumper stickers.

3. Several of these articles contend that the media's obsession with perfect bodies is unhealthy for men and women both physically and psychologically. Some articles point out that earlier generations of feminists argued that we'd all be better off in this society if women simply adopted the attitudes that men held until recently—namely, you can't fight nature, aging, and genes. Instead, women and, increasingly, men are held to unrealistic standards. (As you likely realize, at the same time that we, as a society, seem increasingly concerned with getting and maintaining the perfect body, study after study shows that more Americans than ever before are overweight as defined by the medical profession.) What, in your opinion, accounts for our society's not choosing what many would argue is the saner position—that a person should accept her or his body and not fret about it? What would society be like if that attitude were widespread? Why do more Americans weigh more than they should, from the current medical point of view, precisely at the time when pressure to "look good" grows. Write an essay in which you explore at least one of these questions. To prepare for this assignment, you may want to talk to at least five different people (preferably people of different backgrounds in some way) and ask for their opinions about these matters.

CHAPTER 22

How Does the Media
Stereotype *You*?

Through the media—newspapers, magazines, radio, television, films, and the Internet—we are constantly presented with stereotypes of various groups in our society. Whether based in some degree of reality or not, these stereotypes become part of our cultural folklore, and many people's perceptions of ethnic and social groups are based solely on representations they see in the media. How do we know when a representation will be accepted as tongue-in-cheek, ironic, or offensive or even perceived as true?

- Do the media represent people as ideal types—that is, as we wish we were or as others (marketers? groups with various kinds of social power?) wish we were? If so, to what extent are these practices harmful? To whom? Why?
- Do the media represent some segments of the population in terms of ideal types and other segments in terms of stereotypes? (If so, to what extent are these practices damaging? To whom? Why?
- When do the media influence us directly? When are they mediated in some way—that is, linked to complex changes that, in turn, influence attitudes or behaviors?

Making a Visual Argument: Artists and Comics Take On Stereotyping

Geo Vittoratos, *Come as Your Favorite Stereotype*

Latino Comedy Project, *Will Stereotype for Food*

New York Arab-American *The Arabs Are*
Comedy Festival *Coming!*   pp. 636–639

1. What arguments are being made in each of these images? What sorts of background knowledge must readers bring to the images

to fully understand these arguments? (You'll need to check out the Web site for the New York Arab-American Comedy, <http://arab-comedy.org/news/article_118.shtml>, in order to understand some of the poster's humor and its argument.) How does each image represent an argument about stereotypes in the media and popular culture?

The first image is of a Japanese geisha, a stereotype of Asian feminine beauty. The argument is that this image is an outdated stereotype. By using this image, the artist is pointing out that even this beautiful portrayal of a Japanese woman is a stereotype. The second image, "Will stereotype for food," mocks the stereotype that Latinos come to the United States for welfare benefits and argues that the comics have much to offer. The Arab comedy poster uses the line "The Arabs are coming!" to announce an upcoming show with a phrase that suggests that Arabs are dangerous. This announcement pokes fun at stereotypes that Arabs are enemies of America.

2. Choose one of these arguments, and explain how the visual image contributes to the argument it makes. Try to comment specifically on the elements of the image that support the argument. If you're having trouble getting started, simply consider the text of any of the arguments without the visual image.

Answers will vary.

3. Dressing up as a stereotype for a costume party or stereotyping for food (or even laughs) can be risky business. What's at stake if one performs in some way the stereotypes of a group of which he or she is a member? Of a group of which he or she is not a member? Why are the stakes so different? Must such performances always be humorous? Will they necessarily be offensive? Why or why not?

It is much easier to focus on humor when stereotyping one's own culture. Performing a stereotype of another culture is likely to be seen as racist. Both situations are likely to offend someone. Some people use the stereotypes without humor, and even when the intention is humorous, the basis for the humor may be found to have racist assumptions.

4. Writing assignment

Ethnic minorities are not the only ones who find themselves stereotyped in the media. Choose a group—other than an ethnic minority—that you believe is often negatively portrayed in the media. Describe the kinds of negative portrayals that occur, and speculate on the origins and significance of such portrayals. Give some thought to the effects that these representations have in society at large.

Tania Ralli *Who's a Looter? In the Storm's Aftermath, Pictures Kick Up a Different Kind of Tempest* pp. 640–643

1. In what ways does this controversy hinge on a definitional argument? (For a discussion of arguments of definition, see Chapter 8.) What are the relevant terms, and how are they being defined by various parties?

   The primary conflict of the debate is whether there is a standard definition of *looter* or if race plays into the definition. According to the Associated Press, a looter must be seen entering a business and leaving with goods. Graythen used the verb *carrying* rather than *looting* because he had not seen the couple enter a business.

   Whose definition(s) do you prefer? Why?

   Answers will vary.

2. If the situation Ralli describes is no more than a definitional argument, why was there such controversy? In other words, what, beyond definitions, is or was at stake in this situation?

   Beyond the question of semantics, this debate came to represent the race issues underlying all discussions of New Orleans in the aftermath of Hurricane Katrina. The fear is the young African American man in Stokes's article was labeled as a looter because of his race, or even that the white man and woman were not labeled as such only because of their race.

   How are these larger issues related to the topic of this chapter? How are they related to differing perceptions of American history and of American society at the present time?

Different racial or ethnic groups often see a historic event from different points of view. One side sometimes claims that the other is being ignorant, calculating, or reactionary.

3. As the headnote states, the captions of these two photos were the subject of considerable controversy. Here is a posting by Chris Graythen, who photographed the white couple, on a message board from Sports Shooter, a Web site for sports photographers, <http://sportsshooter.com/message_display.html?tid=17204>. This message was posted on August 31, 2005 at 6:10 p.m. as part of a heated discussion entitled "Finding vs. Looting (word choice in AP caption)." It's reprinted here as it was posted:

Jesus, I don't belive how much crap I'm getting from this. First of all, I hope you excuse me, but I'm completely at the end of my rope. You have no idea how stressful this whole disaster is, espically since I have not seen my wife in 5 days, and my parents and grand parents HAVE LOST THEIR HOMES. As of right now, we have almost NOTHING.

Please stop emailing me on this one.

I wrote the caption about the two people who 'found' the items. I believed in my opinion, that they did simply find them, and not 'looted' them in the definition of the word. The people were swimming in chest deep water, and there were other people in the water, both white and black. I looked for the best picture. there were a million items floating in the water - we were right near a grocery store that had 5+ feet of water in it. it had no doors. the water was moving, and the stuff was floating away. These people were not ducking into a store and busting down windows to get electronics. They picked up bread and cokes that were floating in the water. They would have floated away anyhow. I wouldn't have taken in, because I wouldn't eat anything that's been in that water. But I'm not homeless. (well, technically I am right now.)

I'm not trying to be politically correct. I'm don't care if you are white or black. I spent 4 hours on a boat in my parent's neighborhood shooting, and rescuing people, both black and white, dog and cat. I am a journalist, and a human being - and I see all as such. If you don't belive me, you can look on Getty today and see the images I shot of real looting today, and you will see white and black people, and they were DEFINATELY looting. And I put that in the caption.

Please, please don't argue symantics over this one. This is EX-TREMELY serious, and I can't even begin to convey to those not here what it is like. Please, please, be more concerned on how this affects all of us (watch gas prices) and please, please help out if you can.

This is my home, I will hopefully always be here. I know that my friends in this business across the gulf south are going through the exact same thing - and I am with them, and will do whatever I can to help. But please, please don't email me any more about this caption issue.

And please, don't yell at me about spelling and grammar. Im eating my first real meal (a sandwich) right now in 3 days.

When this calms down, I will be more than willing to answer any questions, just ask.

Thank you all -

-Chris Graythen

What sorts of appeals — ethical, logical, and emotional — does Graythen offer his fellow photographers? Do his mistakes in typing and spelling contribute or detract to his argument and his ethos? Why?

Graythen appeals to his audience on an ethical and logical basis as he explains why he chose the title he did. He then moves to an emotional appeal, stating that important issues will be taking his attention in the near future and encouraging people to concentrate on helping those in need.

4. Writing assignment

Classroom Exercise: focus on the world

In a world where race is an emotional topic for many people, newspaper headlines, evening news reports, or politicians' sound bites frequently contain a phrase or word that offends an ethnic or a cultural group. How do you feel about the debates that ensue after such situations? Must we be more careful about what we say and how we say it? Should we all become less sensitive — and is this easier to suggest when one is not a member of a historically oppressed group? If you were asked to revise the Associated Press style manual in response to media coverage of Hurricane Katrina in New Orleans, what changes would you suggest? What guidelines would you create to avoid a situation like the one described in this selection?

Chong-suk Han *Gay Asian-American Male*
                    Seeks Home   pp. 644–648

1. In his essay, Han is making a general argument about stereotypes in the media and popular culture using gay Asian American males as his example. What specific factors does Han cite that shape the experience of gay Asian American males? How are these men doubly marginalized?

   As gay men in the Asian American community and as Asian men in the American community, gay Asian males are doubly marginalized. Han cites that many gay Asian American males prefer white partners, which means they are competing for a small population of gay white men that prefer Asian men. Han claims that Asian American men are not fully accepted in either the gay community or the Asian American community.

2. Analyze Han's opening paragraph. How does he use the quotation from David Henry Hwang's *M. Butterfly* and the description of responses to a then-recent issue of *Details* magazine to set up his argument? What, specifically, is the importance of his characterization of the French lieutenant, who loved Song Linling, in terms of the former's inability to see the latter as "anything other than a woman"? What's the importance of Han's contrast of the responses of the Asian American and gay community to the feature in *Details?*

   Han argues that Americans are unable to see Asian men as anything other than feminine or gay. He highlights that while the Asian community reacted strongly to the details article, the gay community remained silent.

3. No doubt you rightly assumed that *Gay & Lesbian Review Worldwide* targets lesbians and gay men as its primary audience. In what ways has Han taken that audience into account as he writes? How would you describe his intended audience? His invoked audience?

   Throughout his essay, Han addresses his audience by using jargon (like freedom rings) that is related to the gay com-

munity. His invoked audience is gay Asian American males, but his intended audience seems to be the gay and lesbian community at large.

Given Han's claims, how would you expect issues confronting gay Asian American women to be similar from those confronting gay Asian American males? How might they differ? Do these similarities and differences account sufficiently for Han's focus uniquely on the situation of Asian American men?

Answers will vary.

4. Han contends that the larger gay community's idea of physical beauty is Eurocentric in nature (paragraph 9). What does he see as the consequences of such a situation? In what ways does David Carr's piece, "On Covers of Many Magazines, a Full Racial Palette Is Still Rare" (p. 649), make a similar argument about American society more generally?

Han states that the consequence of a Eurocentric standard of beauty is that gay Asian American men feel themselves to be less than their peers and may be more likely to accept relationships where they are not respected. Carr is arguing that minorities do not see themselves on magazine covers because editors are afraid to alienate their white readers with a model that doesn't fit European beauty standards.

Do you agree or disagree? Why?

Answers will vary.

5. Writing assignment

Classroom Exercise: focus on the world

Are gay Asian males the only ones "seeking a home"? What aspects of the difficulties faced by gay Asian men might be faced by other people who find themselves lonely at the intersection of two minority groups (for example, Deaf and Native Americans or Jewish and Latina Americans)? In the library or on the Internet, research another "double minority" to see what information you can find in the form of Web pages, blogs, essay, or articles. From your search, try to create a list of specific problems that this group faces. How do these problems compare to the issues described in Han's article?

David Carr *On Covers of Many Magazines,*
a Full Racial Palette Is Still Rare pp. 649–653

1. What argument is being made in Carr's article? Does it surprise you in any way? Does it matter that the article appeared in the business section of the newspaper rather than, say, on the front page or in the lifestyle section? Why or why not? How might the argument have been framed differently if it had been written for a different section of the newspaper. Why?

   Carr claims that fashion and women's magazines have generally shunned minority cover models, while teen magazines have embraced a wide spectrum of cover models.

2. What sorts of arguments does Carr use to support his thesis? Certainly consider the kinds of evidence discussed in Chapter 16, but don't limit yourself to these sorts of support.

   Answers will vary, but they should note that Carr uses interviews with magazine editors, quotes from authors of books about media and race, and a visual collage of *Cosmopolitan* covers.

   For example, how does Carr use figurative language (for example, "a ghetto of music and sports magazines," paragraph 12) to advance his argument?

   Carr's use of the term *ghetto* encourages the reader to think of magazine covers in terms of racial and economic disparity. The term refers here to impoverished, mostly African American, inner-city neighborhoods.

3. How do you evaluate Carr's discussion of Black males continuing to end up on the covers of sports and music magazines and of the growing number of "exotic" women who appear on the covers of magazines designed for primarily young White men? Do these facts serve as evidence of "progress"? In what sense? Might they be interpreted in other ways?

   Answers will vary. While these examples can be seen as progress because they mean statistically greater percentages of covers with minority models, they are good illustrations of why sheer numbers don't always tell the whole story. Consider a discussion of how these covers actually maintain the status quo by arguing, for instance, that non-

white women should be seen as different, "other," "exotic," and therefore not "normal" or "the girl-next-door."

4. Writing assignment

Classroom Exercise: focus on the world

Halle Berry made a big stir at the Seventy-fourth Academy Awards in 2002 when she became the first African American woman to win the Oscar for best actress. The issues that David Carr addresses reach beyond magazine covers and into most forms of media representation. Choose a specific media format or genre — for example, a television network, a local nightly news broadcast, prime-time sitcoms, soap operas, reality television shows, courtroom shows (like *Judge Judy* or *Divorce Court*), newspaper advertisements, romantic comedies, or horror films. Using Carr's research as a model, analyze the racial and ethnic makeup of the actors, broadcasters, contestants, models, and so on. How do your results compare with Carr's? Did your results affirm your expectations or surprise you? Do you think any changes should be made to the racial or ethnic makeup of your chosen format? If so, what changes would you suggest? If not, why not?

Commercial   *Mainstream/Business-to-Business*
Closet Association *Advertising Best Practices*   pp. 654–658

1. How would you characterize the arguments being made on this Web page?

   The argument on this Web page is that gay, lesbian, bisexual, and transgender people should be portrayed in the media as normal people in traditional settings and should not be stereotyped.

   Do any of the suggestions or recommendations surprise you? Why or why not? Do they represent common sense or something more?

   Answers will vary.

2. Visit the Web site for this selection, <http://commercialcloset.org/cgi-bin/iowa/index.html?page=best>. Why is this Web site organized as it is? In other words, why are the parts of the site arranged in the order they are? Why are the sections so labeled? How does each section contribute to the Web page's overall argument?

The Web page guides the reader through an explanation of the goals for media presentation of the GLBT communities and addresses issues surrounding implementation stage by stage. Each section addresses possible questions that might arise at each stage.

If you take the intended audience to be advertisers seeking advice on how to market to the gay, lesbian, bisexual, or transgender communities or their friends and supporters, how persuasive is the information provided? Why? How effective do you find the layout and navigability of the Web site?

Answers will vary.

3. Visit the "Best Practices" section of the Web site for this selection, <http://commercialcloset.org/cgi-bin/iowa/index.html?page=best>, which includes links to numerous ads that represent members of the GLBT community. Choose two ads that you think are especially effective, and analyze the kinds of appeals used in these ads. Why do you find that the appeals used are appropriate, given the target audience(s) and the rhetorical goals of the ad?

Answers will vary.

4. Writing assignment

Classroom Exercise: focus on the world

Is America ready for the kind of advertising that the Commercial Closet suggests? Which of its guidelines do you see broken on a regular basis? Which do you think would be hardest for the industry to follow? In groups or pairs, write a commercial script or draw an idea for a print ad that you think would fall within the guidelines that the Web document presents. Discuss in class the specific guidelines that helped shape your idea, and share your ideas with the class.

Anne-Marie O'Connor *Not Only Natalee Is Missing: Is the Media's Inattention to Missing Women Who Aren't White Due to Deliberate Racism or Unconscious Bias?* pp. 659–662

1. What sorts of analyses (arguments, really) do Richard Blair, Todd Boyd, Mark Effron, Andrew Kohut, Katherine Fitzpatrick, and

Maria Len-Rios, Erin Bruno, and Marty Kaplan offer with respect to why women of color are underrepresented in stories of missing women? To what extent do their analyses overlap or complement one another? Are any of the positions they represent as a group contradictory?

Blair states that he believes that the race and the economic status of the missing are factors, and Boyd notes that there is an unconscious division about who matters and who doesn't. Kohut agrees that the public is drawn to what is happening in the lives of the rich and famous. For Fitzpatrick, the public and the media have an idealized picture of a damsel in distress, and people who fit that picture make it into the news. Effron, of MSNBC, says that the involvement of the family in getting the word out helps the media decide which missing women will be covered in news stories. Len-Rios points to the lack of minorities in the newsroom as an issue. Bruno expands on that point, remarking that journalists often look for a story that they themselves can relate to.

Which argument(s) do you find most convincing? Why?

Answers will vary.

2. Andrew Kohut, in particular, focuses on the ways in which cable news networks, borrowing techniques from the tabloid press, go for particular kinds of stories (paragraph 23). Can you give examples of other genres of stories favored by cable networks that have influenced mainstream news programs in your area?

Answers will vary.

3. Erin Bruno contends that reporters may be choosing stories with their audiences in mind (paragraph 30). If audiences, (aside from those of niche channels like Black Entertainment Network or Univision) are majority white, should members of other groups simply accept as fact the idea that their concerns won't be represented in the mainstream media?

Answers will vary.

What are the disadvantages of such a situation for those from minority groups? From the majority group?

The disadvantage for minorities is that their stories will get less attention and less help if the goal is to motivate the com-

**munity or disseminate information. The majority commu-
nity will have a skewed idea of what is happening in their
larger communities and country. There may be issues or opportunities missed by an uninformed white community.**

4. O'Connor uses several sources of information or kinds of evidence
to support her claims. What are they?

**O'Connor uses interviews, news examples, and statistics to
support her argument.**

How effective are they?

Answers will vary.

How would the article be different if she had used far more statistics and far less interview data? Would it be more or less effective?
Why? (For a discussion of kinds of evidence, see Chapter 16.)

**With more statistics and fewer interviews, the disparity of
reporting might have been more obvious, but the interviews provide an inside view into the media.**

5. Writing assignment

Classroom Exercise: focus on the world

How much of what we see in the news is influenced by the people
who own the media? The people who work in the media? The preferences of viewers? Are "viewers" the population at large or a targeted
segment of viewers? Do different networks or media outlets focus on
different populations? What do we miss when news is selectively presented or presented with bias? Can news really be presented without
bias? How can choices for news coverage be made objectively?

David Bositis *Skin-Deep: What Polls of
Minorities Miss*   pp. 663–666

1. How would you summarize Bositis's argument?

**Bositis argues that opinion polls in the United States leave
out minorities and therefore that the minority perspective
is underrepresented to the peril of public knowledge.**

In what ways is it an evaluative argument? A proposal argument?
What proposal might he be making? Why?

The argument is an evaluative one because Bositis discusses what is lacking in current polling methodologies. It is also a proposal argument because Bositis states that polling operations should seek out minority opinion even though it can cost more, pollsters should be of the same ethnic group as their intended community, and polls should focus on local communities to gain better understanding at the smallest levels.

2. What are the challenges of polling minority communities adequately?. Paragraphs 6 and 7 give specific problems pollsters face with respect to minority communities. Why do these problems arise?

Because minority communities are small, more effort must be made to find appropriate interviewees. Moreover, not all minority populations speak English. The extra effort means more cost for the polling operation. These difficulties arise from the size of minority communities and cultural differences, such as language.

What are the public policy implications of polling minority communities? Of not doing so? How might not doing so contribute to stereotypes of minority communities?

Making an effort to poll minorities means that the population can be represented in its entirety with fewer gaps and misunderstandings. Without minority voices, some opinions are left unreported, and stereotypes may continue to survive if minority voices are not heard to dispel those misunderstandings.

3. Does this essay hold any clues to Bositis's own political beliefs?

Bositis makes it clear that he thinks that minorities are ignored in collecting data on public opinion and that the current practices lead to misunderstandings and lack of trust between communities.

If so, what are those clues? How would you characterize the ethos Bositis creates for himself?

The author's ethos is one of informed opinion and stoic activist. He presents himself as a credible source by using statistical examples.

4. Visit the Web sites of the Pew Research Center for the People and the Press or the Tomas Rivera Policy Institute to find out the sorts of research these institutions support with respect to minority communities in the United States. How does such research support an understanding of the changing nature of American society?

   Answers will vary.

5. Writing assignment

Classroom Exercise: focus on the world

Selections from this chapter have addressed the lack of minority representation in magazine images, missing persons stories, and opinion polls. These articles taken together seem to create an even stronger argument for the media's general lack of concern for minority populations. Compare the three pieces, and identify common themes or claims that tie the arguments together.

William Sea *Advertising Sets Double Standard for the Male Gender*   pp. 667–668

1. How might we summarize Sea's argument? What sorts of causal claims does he make? What sorts of evaluative claims does he make?

   Sea's argument is that sexist stereotypes in advertising attack men just as much as women. He states that manly commercials are a backlash against metrosexual presentations of men, and through examples, he evaluates the state of advertising.

   How well are they supported?

   Answers will vary.

2. The Miller commercial engages in what some researchers term *gender policing,* that is, seeking out and punishing behaviors that don't reflect prescribed gender roles and stereotypes. How does such policing perpetuate stereotypes? Can you think of policing that occurs with other groups—for example, members of ethnic groups, lesbians and gay men, religious believers, and political partisans?

The policing of certain behaviors perpetuates stereotypes by delineating the actions that fall outside of socially acceptable male or female personas. This happens with members of many subgroups of the population, such as when a young man is told that he isn't acting black enough or straight enough.

What functions does such policing serve? What are its disadvantages?

Such policing limits the acceptable behaviors for a specific group in an effort to subdue change and disallow variation. One disadvantage is that people who do not conform are made to feel unwelcome. Another disadvantage is that others may conform simply to be accepted.

3. What function does "then" serve in the first sentence of paragraph 5? In what way might Sea be seen as stereotyping feminists and their responses to sexism in advertising?

    The "then" in paragraph 6 is used to connect to the causes in the previous chapter. It also seems to be leveled at all feminists, which creates another dangerous stereotype, as all feminists would not necessarily disagree with Sea and his argument.

    What does this sentence tell us about Sea's invoked readers and their beliefs? (For a discussion of invoked readers, see Chapter 1.)

    Sea's invoked readers are feminists who have not considered that stereotypes of males in advertising are just as powerful and damaging as the stereotypes of women.

4. Writing assignment

Classroom Exercise: focus on the world

What might Sea and Guy Trebay ("When Did Skivvies Get Rated NC-17?" in Chapter 21) agree on about the double standard for males? How are social pressures different for males and females? Why might certain advertising campaigns resort to old gender-role stereotypes, while others take advantage of sexualizing the male body even for masculine products?

The Onion *Graphic Artist Carefully Assigns Ethnicities to Anthropomorphic Recyclables* pp. 669–671

1. Does *The Onion* live up to its claim? In other words, is this article satirical? If it is, what things are being satirized and how? (For a discussion of satire, see Chapter 13.) The essay likewise employs irony. What, for example, is ironic about Heather Franks's closing remarks about the soda can (paragraph 15)?

   The Onion is satirizing the level of political correctness that government institutions often attempt to achieve in an effort not to offend anyone. Also satirized is the attitude of the artist who is more worried about breaking an obvious stereotype than actually offending anyone. The irony here is that the soda can that is going to be put in charge—because everyone just has feeling about him—is white.

2. Do you find this essay amusing? Funny? Did it make you laugh? What might account for your response?

   Answers will vary.

3. A photo of Chrissie Bellisle, the imaginary graphic artist mentioned in the text, appeared with the original article. We did not seek permission to use it (for issues around in intellectual property, see Chapter 18) but believe it's relevant that Bellisle is white—or appears to be. Why might *The Onion* have included a photo of Chrissie Bellisle? What role would it play for readers? is it better to be told Bellisle's apparent ethnicity or to be presented with a photo of her? Why?

   Showing a picture of the fictional artist lends a bit of reality to the piece, and choosing a white model for the picture may play into the racial situation of the story.

4. How does a satiric piece like this one contribute to an understanding of stereotypes in the media and popular culture? What does the goal of this argument seem to be?

   In the most overt sense, the author may list stereotypes by describing the artist's abandoned pieces that might be offensive. All the possibly offensive combinations support the fact that there really are many offensive stereotypes at work in our society. The goal of the argument seems to be to show how sensitive we need to be but also how politi-

cally correct someone can be without really caring about the damage of the stereotype itself. After all, the artist is drawing garbage.

5. Writing assignment

Classroom Exercise: focus on the world

This piece of satire invites the readers to consider the stereotypes in our culture and also our reactions to such stereotypes. How do we go about fighting stereotypes or changing perceptions? In the end, even after arduous deliberation and deliberate "balance," will the majority population prevail as does the artist's soda can, which she describes as white? How often is our avoidance of stereotypes an effort to be politically correct rather than truly empathetic and genuine? How often have you seen in the media the sort of images that the article makes fun of? Are people unaware? Are they flouting political correctness? Are they "just having fun"? Or are some of these stereotypes still held firmly in the beliefs of some media producers? Is there an appreciative audience for such stereotypes in film and advertising? Is there or should there be a best-practices guide for minority representation in the media?

Wrap-up Exercises for Constructing Arguments about Stereotypes and the Media

The following questions invite students to consider themes from the readings in this cluster. They can be used for extended projects as well as in-class essay questions.

1. Write a personal response to one or both of the topics of the two clusters in this chapter: representation of the body or stereotypes of groups. (In a recent issue of *Cosmopolitan*, for example, the only heavy women we saw were in an ad for cleaning products, and the ad showed far more women of color than the remainder of the magazine did. In other words, part of the stereotyping of ethnic minorities involves the representation of women's bodies.) In your response, detail your understanding of the impact of images in the media on your own life. Do you see yourself and people like you (in any sort of way) represented in the media? If you do, where? How often? In what sorts of roles or situations? What are the consequences of these facts for you? For those like you? For

those who are not like you? If you do not see yourself or others like you (in any sort of way) represented in the media, what are the consequences of that fact for you? For others like you? For those who are not like you?

2. This chapter explores whether the media stereotype certain categories of Americans—especially ethnic minorities but even groups such as fathers. Many of the readings in this cluster assert that the people seen most often in the media are those who are beautiful and thin. Write an essay in which you examine the potential consequences of this situation for society as a whole and for various groups in society. (Perhaps you will wish to argue that there are no negative consequences of this situation or that if there are, we should not be concerned with them.) Your essay will likely be most successful if you are careful to qualify your claims and to cite specific evidence, rather than dealing in vague generalities.

CHAPTER 23

Is Sports Just a Proxy for Politics?

The readings in this chapter address topics that students often do not consider—the ways in which financial concerns and social and political issues are always present in matters of sports. The goal of the readings and the chapter is not to complain about these facts in a naïve way. It should be clear that our national identity and even our national contentions or difficulties become evident in our discussions about sports. From such a perspective, the readings prompt us to ask questions like these:

- What sorts of larger issues are involved in our preferred leisure-time activities? Why are these issues frequently examined at this particular time?
- What are the advantages and disadvantages of collegiate athletics as they currently are structured? Who or what profits, and who (if anyone) loses or suffers because of the economics of college athletics (or any leisure-time activity)? What is lost? Are the consequences immediate only, or might they be long-term? What are the profits and losses of players, spectators, owners, and sponsors, and how do they shift over time? Is the emerging balance good? Why or why not? (Similar questions can be asked about product placement in movies and television or corporate sponsorship of music festivals and cultural events.)
- Is it possible to think about gender equality in college athletics from a gain/gain perspective? What factors lead us to see college athletics programs as winners and losers, as we so often do? If no other remedy to the history of unequal opportunity can be found, are there ways of weighing reduced opportunities for specific men in particular cases against the potential long-term benefits of women's participation in sports?

Juliet Macur *Rowing Scholarships Available.*
No Experience Necessary   pp. 675–680

1. Macur's article is clearly intended to be a news article. What sorts of arguments can it be said to make? Why?

   The need for colleges to spend equal amounts of money on men and women athletes has opened up scholarship and competition opportunities for women who had never before seriously considered sports.

2. According to Macur, the popularity of rowing as a varsity sport for women has little to do with the appeal of rowing itself. What accounts for its popularity? Why does it appeal to athletic directors at major universities, which generally have large football teams and men's basketball teams?

   Title IX has forced schools with large football programs to expand sports opportunities for women to balance spending on men's and women's sports. Rowing is a popular choice for schools looking to fund women's sports because it requires many athletes to enter competitions.

   Why does it appeal to collegiate women?

   Recruitment for rowing means an opportunity to try a new sport and more scholarships for female rowers.

3. Ads like those from *The Daily Texan* are common in the fall, at least at large universities like those mentioned in question 2. What kinds of arguments do they make?

   These ads present an argument that female athletes are in demand and that this is a positive opportunity for female students.

   What are the advantages of such ads? Are there any disadvantages?

   The ads reach women who might not have considered these sports before, help to fill the roster, and might persuade some promising athletes to attend the meetings. Advertising that is openly targeted for women could draw negative backlash from the student body.

4. As noted in the headnote, Macur's article appeared under two different titles in different editions of the *New York Times*. The titles

were "Rowing Scholarships Available. No Experience Necessary" and "Never Rowed? Take a Free Ride." What does the first title remind you of? What sort of word play does the second contain?

The first title is reminiscent of "help wanted" posters. The second title uses the ambiguous "free ride" to imply riding in a boat or receiving a scholarship for college.

Which do you find to be more effective? Why?

Answers will vary.

5. What might be the benefits of introducing women who haven't previously been involved in team sports to sports like rowing?

Women who have not been involved in sports may develop a previously undiscovered talent, and sports may bring new levels of self-esteem and even better personal health to young women.

Are there any disadvantages?

Some may argue that if team rosters are filled with first-time athletes, then the competitive level may lower, creating a waste of money. Coaches of smaller men's sports may argue that that money should be going to their more promising male athletes.

6. Writing assignment

Classroom Exercise: focus on the argument

Reading Macur's report, can you find any evidence of the author's own personal stance on Title IX and its ramifications? Using the data in the argument as a basis, have students construct an argument for or against Title IX as if they were trying to convince Macur of their own opinion. These arguments can be shared in class or used as a platform for class debate.

Jessica Gavora *Time's Up for Title IX Sports*   pp. 681–689

1. This selection promises "to tell the truth about Title IX" (paragraph 10). What, in Gavora's eyes, is the truth? What specific arguments does she make against Title IX?

Gavora feels that Title IX is "an attempt to dictate how men and women should behave" and is a government-enforced quota system.

How persuasive are they?

Answers will vary.

2. What sorts of evidence does Gavora use in constructing her argument? (For a discussion of what counts as evidence, see Chapter 16.)

She includes inartistic proofs such as statistical evidence and reports from schools that have been affected by the law, and she includes artistic proofs such as analogies to past instances of discrimination.

Unlike the previous reading, which offers an argument in the form of information and facts, Gavora's argument is explicitly combative. Who are the readers that her text invokes (see Chapter 1)? What values does she assume they have?

Gavora invokes an audience of conservative readers who are opposed to gender quotas, to an activist federal government, and to gender discrimination.

3. What is Gavora's attitude toward feminism? How do you know? How does this attitude manifest itself in this essay?

While Gavora acknowledges the accomplishments of feminism in the past, she is generally hostile to the current feminist movement; she writes, for instance, that feminism took a "destructive turn" and that liberals made the movement for women's equality "a separatist movement."

What does she concede about the role that conservatives have traditionally taken toward women's rights (paragraph 31 and following)?

She concedes that conservatives did not support women's equality and also that "more often than not they resisted it."

Does this concession strengthen or weaken her argument? Why?

Answers will vary.

4. As mentioned in the headnote, Gavora seeks to discredit not only Title IX but also its supporters. How effective do you find her use of this rhetorical strategy? Why?

Answers will vary.

Why is it a risky strategy?

It might appear to some readers that Gavora is straying from the argument of the Title IX ruling itself or that she is making personal attacks.

5. Writing assignment

Classroom Exercise: focus on the argument

Every argument has its opposing viewpoints. How might someone oppose Gavora's argument? Map the possible points of opposition. What kind of evidence would someone need to present to argue effectively against Gavora's claims?

Ruth Conniff *Title IX: Political Football*   pp. 690–695

1. What arguments is Conniff putting forth about Title IX?

Title IX is good for girls who play sports, for the families (especially fathers) of these girls, and for the culture of sports. She also argues that Title IX is currently under attack because people are unwilling to blame football, the real cause of sports funding troubles.

What argument, in particular, is she making in the concluding section of her essay (paragraphs 22–27)?

That Title IX is under attack in part because it has been successful in increasing the athletic opportunities for women, leading some to argue that the law is no longer needed.

How well do you think she supports her claims? Why?

Answers will vary.

2. Conniff chooses carefully the sources she cites, especially with regard to quotations likely based on interviews. (For additional information on kinds of evidence such as interviews, see Chapter 16.) In paragraph 5, for example, she quotes Joe Kelly, a father, as claiming that Title IX "is one of the best things that ever happened

to fathers." Later, she quotes Kelly as saying that he and other members of Dads and Daughters "are not radical feminists" (paragraph 7). In paragraph 16, she quotes Donna Shalala, "one of the nation's biggest boosters of Title IX—and of big-budget football." Why are such details and characterizations important in the argument Conniff is constructing?

Conniff needs to personalize the story of Title IX. She quotes people (the wrestling coach, a chancellor who supports big-time football, a father) who might be expected to be Title IX opponents but who end up not blaming Title IX for the cuts in men's sports programs.

In countering arguments put forth by people like Jessica Gavora in the previous selection?

One argument that is especially important for countering Gavora might be that men—particularly the fathers of female athletes—are important beneficiaries of Title IX. This effect shows that the law benefits both sexes and that it can help strengthen families, an appeal that might be effective with conservative readers.

3. Notice the ways that Conniff's word choice supports her argument. Look back at the text to find several instances of effective word choice, including figurative language, and state why you think they are effective. (For additional information on figurative language, see Chapter 12.) How does word choice contribute to Conniff's ethos as an author? As an authority?

Answers will vary.

4. Writing assignment

Classroom Exercise: focus on rhetoric

The introduction to this article and several of the questions encourage students to pay close attention to Conniff's word choice and style. Take this exercise a step further: have students choose a paragraph to rewrite in a different style. They can be more or less descriptive or change the vocabulary in the paragraph to be more or less formal, for instance. How do the new paragraphs compare to the original? What does Conniff's style do effectively? Where can you improve on her choices?

Leslie Heywood *Despite the Positive Rhetoric about*
Women's Sports, Female Athletes
Face a Culture of Sexual
Harassment pp. 696–701

1. What solutions does Heywood recommend for eliminating the sexual abuse and harassment of female athletes by coaches? Do you think her proposal is viable? Why or why not?

   She advocates seminars and training programs for coaches and athletes, administered from within athletics departments rather than by other offices, to educate them about rights and responsibilities. She also mentions orientation sessions for parents on the potential social dangers their athlete daughters may face. She calls for a change in traditional sports culture that values male athletes as "the real thing" and trivializes problems such as harassment as distractions to winning. Heywood also urges parents and athletes to seek out schools that have protections such as those mentioned above for their female athletes.

2. The first two paragraphs of Heywood's article do not directly address the main topic. What is Heywood doing in these paragraphs?

   She is establishing the fact that depression is a serious problem affecting half of all adolescent girls and that sports offer a "major solution to those problems."

   Why does she open the article in this way?

   She is showing that sports are more than just play and that they can contribute a great deal to mental as well as physical health.

   How well does the strategy work?

   Answers will vary.

3. Writing to an audience of educators and policy-making officials of sports organizations such as the NCAA, Heywood uses a combination of personal and statistical evidence to construct her argument. How might she have changed her article for an audience of parents?

   She might have emphasized the role played by parents in affecting university policies or the role parents play in the

recruiting process. She might have mentioned some specific warning signals to watch for in their daughters' behavior. She would likely have relied more on arguments based on the heart.

Of athletes?

She might have talked more about fear of reprisals for whistle-blowing.

How might she alter her appeal in a speech to a coaches' conference?

She might change or delete the discussion of Coach Dorrance because he is so well known and popular and the audience may be defensive on his behalf.

4. In the "Issues and Action" section of the Women's Sports Foundation Web site, <http://womenssportsfoundation.org>, readers can find a document entitled "Addressing the Issue of Verbal, Physical and Psychological Abuse of Athletes: The Foundation Position." Even if this specific document isn't available when you're using this textbook, there are likely documents on similar topics on the Women's Sports Foundation Web site. Examine the information included in a relevant document, comparing and contrasting it with Heywood's argument. How are they similar? How are they different?

Answers will vary.

5. Writing assignment

Classroom Exercise: focus on the world

This exercise is likely to be quite volatile, but it can provide a good opportunity for exploration of ideas. In addition, by periodically leading students' attention back to their methods of argumentation, the exercise can give students practice in rhetorical strategy. Open discussion with the following questions: What courses of action are available to women athletes who are experiencing sexual harassment from a coach? Evaluate the options. What would be the preferred action? Why? How, if at all, would it be different for a male athlete? Why? (There are really four potential combinations to explore here: female athlete/male coach, female athlete/female coach, male athlete/male coach, male athlete/female coach.) How, if at all, would it be different if an episode of serious harassment occurred on the eve of a championship game or series? Why?

Barbara Munson *Common Themes and Questions about the Use of "Indian" Logos* pp. 702–708

1. What's Munson's argument? Why is it stated where and as it is? How might her purpose in writing have led her to organize her material in this way?

Munson's argument, which opens the selection, is that the use of Indian logos promotes racism. Stating this thesis succinctly at the beginning of the manifesto leaves readers with no question about what they can expect as they read.

Would the selection have been more or less effective if she'd organized her argument as a "regular" essay, consisting of an introduction that leads to her thesis statement, several paragraphs of a body, and a conclusion? Why or why not?

The presentation of point and counterpoint guides the readers through the piece and addresses the most common defenses of the use of Indian logos. This organization highlights each of the points that Munson refutes and speaks to the reader in a way that a traditional essay would not be able to.

2. Examine the arrangement and organization of the "common questions and statements" to which Munson replies. Why are they arranged in this way? Would her argument be strengthened or weakened if these paragraphs were arranged differently, that is, if they were in a different order?

The organization of the topics adds to the strength of the argument. Munson moves from the most obvious questions to the more difficult questions that people raise about the issue. Ending with a question and response about why schools are reluctant to change their Indian logos shows that Munson is aware of the complicated nature of the debate.

Are there advantages and disadvantages to such implicit organization of an argument?

The advantage to such organization is a smooth flow of ideas throughout the piece. A disadvantage is that the thesis and supports are not presented concisely but rather are re-stated at different times throughout the article.

3. How would you characterize Munson's tone in this selection? Her ethos? What evidence would you cite for your conclusions? How do her tone and ethos contribute to or detract from her argument?

Munson's tone is serious, controlled, and even handed. This tone contributes to an ethos of knowledge and experience, which adds to her argument by creating credibility.

Would you characterize this argument as Rogerian? (For a discussion of Rogerian argumentation, see Chapter 1.) Why or why not?

Answers will vary.

4. One of Munson's concerns is the influence of "Indian" logos on children, both Native American and non-Indian. Do you agree with her argument? Why or why not?

Answers will vary.

How does her mention of children early in the argument add to the weight or gravity of her topic as she defines it?

She argues that racism is persisting. Exposing children — the next generation — to racist views in school negatively affects the future.

5. Although American Indian logos, names, mascots, and symbols show up in many places in popular culture, Munson is concerned specifically with athletics and sports events. Why?

Munson states that the use of Indian logos as part of another culture's games is particularly insulting. Additionally, Indian students face racism and non-Indian students see or participate in racist acts whenever an Indian mascot is displayed. This activity divorces the Indian people from the symbols of their heritage.

In what sense does her article demonstrate that these logos, names, mascots, and symbols have become part of larger political debates?

Some argue that the debate about Indian logos is just an extension of political correctness or minority complaining and don't try to understand the issue.

6. Writing assignment

Classroom Exercise: focus on the argument

Does your university or college use an Indian logo or another ethnic logo? How about students' favorite professional teams? How do students feel about changing these names and mascots? Do they have other suggestion of names and images that satisfactorily represent the spirit of the school? Does changing the mascot somehow break the chain of tradition? Does it change the ethos of the institution? Do people in the community in which the students are studying think that the change would be worth the effort?

Jim Shore *Play with Our Name* pp. 709–711

1. What's Shore's argument?

Shore argues that rather than ban the use of Indian mascots, the NCAA should consider encouraging schools with those mascots to build better relationships with Indian tribes that live near the universities. He uses his own Seminole tribe's experience working with Florida State University as an example of a successful relationship.

What evidence does he offer in support of his claim? In what sense might we say that Shore's argument is Rogerian? (For a discussion of Rogerian argumentation, see Chapter 1.)

Shore acknowledges that some Indian logos are offensive, but he is encouraging a compromise rather than a win for one side or the other. He recommends that schools use less offensive portrayals of Indians and cultivate relationships with the Indian communities near them.

2. In what senses is Shore's argument a proposal argument? (For a discussion of proposal arguments, see Chapter 11.)

Shore proposes an alternative to banning Indian mascots.

Evaluate it as such.

Answers will vary.

3. Shore concedes that the Seminole Tribe receives no direct financial compensation for use of the Seminole name and related symbols. Should it? What would be the advantages or disadvantages of such an arrangement? For whom?

   Answers will vary.

4. Imagine a dialogue between Barbara Munson, author of the previous selection, "Common Themes and Questions about the Use of 'Indian' Logos," and Shore.

   Both authors would probably agree that some mascots, like Sammy the Seminole, are more offensive than others. Munson might even agree that educational materials produced at FSU positively affect the tribal community.

   What things would they likely agree about? Would there be disagreements? If so, what would be the likely source of those disagreements?

   They would likely disagree about the extent to which FSU alumni in Florida state government feel a kindred spirit for the Seminole tribe. Munson would probably argue that FSU students and graduates do not associate actual Indians with their team mascot and that publicity the FSU brings to the tribe is negligible.

5. Writing assignment

Classroom Exercise: focus on rhetoric

Ask students to analyze this text using Toulmin analysis. What are the claims, warrants, grounds, and backing? Where is the argument strongest? Where is it weakest? Do they expect programs of this sort to be effective in aiding Native American communities and combating racism? Why or why not?

Making a Visual Argument: Editorial Cartoonists Take On the Use of Native American Mascots and Imagery

Lucy A. Ganje, *Reality TV*

Lalo Alcaraz, *But I'm Honoring You, Dude!*

Thom Little Moon, *Which One Is the Mascot?*   pp. 712–715

1. Each cartoon is critical of the ways in which American Indians and their culture are appropriated by the larger culture. What argument does each cartoon make, and how, specifically, does it make it?

   Ganje's cartoon presents the argument that defenders of Indian logos are ignoring or not seeking out the vast research that exists about the pejorative effects of Indian logos. She spells out her argument quite clearly. Alcaraz argues that sports fans bring no honor to Indian tribes. His statement is intuited from the slovenly appearance of the fan in the cartoon. Little Moon makes his point by drawing a traditional Indian mascot beside caricatures of other minorities. The juxtaposition carries the message that Indian mascots are just as offensive as any other racist portrayal of a minority group.

2. Which cartoon is most effective with respect to supporting the argument it wishes to make? Why? (Here, you'll need to evaluate the effectiveness of each cartoon in terms of what it seeks to achieve; then, you'll need to compare among these three, choosing the most effective. In other words, you'll be making an evaluative argument, as discussed in Chapter 9.)

   Answers will vary.

3. Cartoons, if effective, are humorous. How does each of these cartoons construct a humorous argument? (For a discussion of how humorous arguments work, see Chapter 13.)

   Ganje relies on the irony of the obvious to create humor. Alcaraz also uses the irony of a fan claiming to honor Indian heritage in his ridiculous outfit and unsightly appearance. This argument also serves as a satire of sports fans who ignore conversations of Indian logos.

4. Examine the other cartoons in the gallery at American Indian Sports Teams Mascots site, <http://www.aistm.org/1indexpage .htm>. Choose the one you believe makes the strongest argument. (You may also wish to find a cartoon on this topic that you believe is effective from another source.) In several paragraphs, describe the cartoon and its contents, the argument it makes, and evaluate it. Write two versions of this assignment. Include the cartoon in one version; in the other, don't include the cartoon but provide a detailed description of it so that the reader can imagine it. After

you've finished both versions, write a paragraph in which you describe the challenges of writing about a visual argument like a cartoon when that argument isn't part of the text itself.

Answers will vary.

5. These cartoons and the Web site from which they come are obviously opposed to the use of American Indian mascots and imagery. In fact, we couldn't locate cartoons—at least not interesting
ones—that took a position opposed to the position illustrated
here. Is it possible to design such a cartoon? Why or why not?

**It is possible to draw such a cartoon, but even those who
support the use of Indian mascots may hesitate to make a
joke of the issue.**

Design a cartoon that supports the use of American Indian mascots
and imagery. (If you feel you have no artistic abilities, you can
write a description of the cartoon you would draw if you could.) If
you can't come up with such a cartoon, write an essay in which
you seek to explain why creating such a cartoon is difficult. In a
real sense, your essay will be definitional in that it defines the reasons why it's challenging or perhaps impossible to create a visual
argument in support of the use of American Indian mascots and
imagery by athletic teams.

Answers will vary.

Thad Williamson *Bad As They Wanna Be*   pp. 716–722

1. What evidence does Williamson provide to support his contention
that "the [college athletics] system is rapidly spinning out of control" (paragraph 5)?

**He is referring to the "commercial values" to which the sys-
tem is succumbing. As evidence, he mentions corporate
logos placed prominently in university arenas and uni-
forms, lucrative TV contracts, and concessions to large
donors.**

What kind of appeals does he use? Arguments from the heart? Arguments of character? Other kinds? (See Chapters 2–4.)

He uses all four kinds, but arguments of value predominate, followed by arguments of character and arguments from the heart.

2. Why does Williamson give us so much detailed information about North Carolina coach Dean Smith's political beliefs?

   He wants to establish North Carolina as a school that, even in athletics, represents ethical action.

   Does that information contribute to the argument? How? Why? If not, why not?

   It works to cast the commercialization of college athletics in a less favorable light.

3. Williamson's article ends with a strong call to action, yet there's no hint of such an appeal in the title or opening paragraphs of the article. Why do you think Williamson chose this rhetorical strategy?

   He may have felt it necessary or desirable to grab readers' attention and sympathy before urging them to action.

4. Do you agree with Williamson's suggestion (in paragraph 16) that collegiate sports are "a way out" for poor and working-class students? Do you think that assertion is more (or less) true today than it was in the past? What evidence would you want to present to support or refute Williamson's claim?

   Answers will vary.

5. Writing assignment

Classroom Exercise: focus on the world

Does your school have commercial contracts for advertisements in sports arenas, auditoriums, or places where students gather? How do you feel about being bombarded by advertising messages? Are there places where you feel advertisements are especially appropriate or inappropriate? Where? Why? Williamson calls for "those who love the game [to] fight to change it" (paragraph 20), but he isn't specific about exactly what people should do. If you think that reducing the commercialization is desirable, what might people do to bring about that change?

Tom Sorensen *Dress Code Suitable Only to*
NBA Suits pp. 723–725

1. In what senses is the NBA Player Dress Code a definitional argument?

   The NBA dress code defines the way that NBA administrators think that a professional sports player should dress. They are therefore creating an argument about the definition of a professional appearance.

   How successful is it as such an argument? Why? (For a discussion of definitional arguments, see Chapter 8.)

   Answers will vary.

2. According to Sorensen, why is the NBA Player Dress Code unnecessary? Which events or circumstances, in particular, does Sorensen see as having led to the creation of a dress code?

   Sorensen argues that the clothing that players wear will not affect their behavior in public, and this is what he sees as the goal of the dress code. If players dress up and calm down, the NBA administrators believe that they can change the NBA's image in the wake of incidents like the fight that broke out in November 2004 at the Auburn Hills, Michigan Palace.

   In what sense can these events be seen as political or as being part of larger political debates in the United States?

   The debate has drawn attention to larger issues of race and class between NBA players and administrators. Some have even leveled accusations of racism at those pushing the dress code. The dress code has been described as white and elitist — an attempt to make players seem less "black" to viewers and wealthy fans.

3. What functions does the opening example of Rae Carruth serve in Sorensen's argument (paragraph 1)?

   Rae Carruth serves as an example that stylish clothes do not make a man a good person.

   Is it important that Sorensen is able to use personal experience here (rather than, say, reporting on something he observed on cable television)? Why or why not?

The fact that Sorensen was at the trial and observed Carruth's clothing and manner each day adds to the argument by creating an ethos of credibility for the author.

4. Writing assignment

Classroom Exercise: focus on the world

Have students research other articles that discuss sports and politics, particularly sports and race. They can start by searching Web sites such as ESPN.com and SportsIllustrated.com. These two media outlets usually assess the state of race in sports every February for Black History Month, but they and other sources publish articles throughout the year. Have sports organizations handled the issue of race differently from the rest of society? Are there any assumptions that carry through sports journalists' writing that surprise you? Do you see evidence of double standards for black and white athletes?

Larry Stewart *Barkley Fully Supports NBA's*
New Dress Code pp. 726–728

1. As noted, Stewart's article focuses on Charles Barkley, but much of the article is devoted to the NBA Player Dress Code. What is Barkley's opinion of the NBA dress code? Why? How does he support his position?

   Barkley has a favorable opinion of the dress code because he says that he sees it as a good business decision. He supports creating a more professional appearance for the league and a better model for young people who emulate the players. Barkley contends that the players have the money to dress better and that he would hire a well dressed white man over a casually dressed black man.

2. To what extent do Barkley and Ted Sorensen, author of the previous selection, see the NBA Dress Code as an effort to respond to similar social forces or issues?

   Sorensen and Barkley both see the dress code as a tool meant to make players seem more refined. Barkley even concedes that there are racial overtones to the proposal.

   To what extent do they see it as an effort to respond to different social forces or issues?

Barkley differs from Sorensen in that he states that the business pressures are stronger than the desire to create a better model for youth.

3. What kind of ethos does Barkley create for himself (with the assistance of Stewart)? How does his former career as a professional basketball player contribute to (or perhaps detract from) that ethos?

   The ethos that Barkley presents is one of experience and wisdom. As a player, he represents someone with an understanding of the current players' point of view, but his current position as a commentator may detract from his position. He could be seen as a businessman who has found a different kind of success and has lost the ability to empathize with NBA players.

4. If you examine a number of responses to the NBA Player Dress Code, you'll find that writers seem to agree that a major issue to be considered is the influence of professional basketball players, many of whom are African American, on young African American boys and men. In what ways is this issue a political one?

   This issue becomes political because the inherent message in the dress code is that the only way to be a good role model is to dress like a professional because dressing any differently projects a negative image. A value judgment is attached to wearing jerseys, jeans, and athletic wear. The question becomes whether the only appropriate role model for young black men is a wealthy professional in business clothing.

5. Writing assignment

Classroom Exercise: focus on the argument

Don't most professional organizations have a dress code? Did students' high schools have dress codes? What about the institution where this class is being taught? Should certain minimum standards of appearance be maintained in institutions or organizations? Have students create what they think would be an acceptable dress code for their school. It could be one that they think would be widely accepted or one that they think would be the most appropriate although perhaps not popular. Compare ideas of a minimum standard with the class to see how similar or different the students' ideas are.

Bryan Curtis *Cheerleaders: What to Do*
about Them?   pp. 729–732

1. What, for Curtis, is "America's cheerleading dilemma" (paragraph 2)? Where, for Curtis, are the origins of this dilemma to be found?

   Curtis describes the dilemma of cheerleading as one of identity crisis. Cheerleading has changed over the last century, while the reputation of the cheerleader has remained fixed in an earlier era.

   How does he link the changing nature of this dilemma to shifting gender politics?

   Cheerleading was once the realm of men but has now become a primarily women's sport. Cheerleading as a women's sport had to pass through a cycle of hypersexualization and recently has been seen as a training ground for future leaders, much the same way that male cheerleading had been viewed.

2. Most readers would likely characterize Curtis's argument as humorous. What sorts of humor does Curtis employ? Give three specific examples of different kinds of humor that he uses, explaining how each kind of humor and each example contributes to Curtis's goals. (For a discussion of humorous arguments, see Chapter 13.)

   Answers will vary.

3. However misdirected some readers may find Al Edwards's efforts to clean up athletic events at Texas high schools, Edwards has hit upon what he perceives as a contradiction: Texas schools, like many in the country, frame sex education in terms of abstinence-only curricula while female cheerleaders generally wear less and less and behave in ways that increasingly resemble the routines of exotic dancers. Do you think that Edwards is correct in his assessment? Why or why not? If you do agree with him, why do you think the contradiction exists and persists? If you do not see a contradiction, why do you think Edwards does?

   Answers will vary.

4. In what ways do arguments about female cheerleaders, their attire, and their routine demonstrate that arguments about sports are, in the end, often arguments about politics in some way? In other words, how do such arguments relate to debates about a range of

topics, many of which are debated among elected officials or various interest groups, in the United states.

Curtis describes efforts to curb cheerleading attire and routines as persecution and suggests that many people take issue with cheerleaders because they perceive them to be sex objects rather than women who are gaining valuable experience for the working world.

5. Writing assignment

Classroom Exercise: focus on the argument

Curtis gives a history of the development of cheerleading, its reputation, and its realities, but he does not take on the issue of sexually explicit dance moves as performed by junior high and high school students. What kinds of routines are performed by cheerleaders or dance teams at the students' home institution? What do students think of sexually provocative routines in sports events in general? At the university and high school level? At what age is it appropriate for young girls to use sexually suggestive moves? Did the students feel differently when they were younger? Should district- or statewide rules be instated, or should the policing be left to coaches, parents, and PTA groups?

Wrap-up Exercises for Constructing Arguments about Sports and Politics

These three exercises are suggested as activities in which students can integrate any or all of the readings of the chapter. In addition, Exercise 1 would be suitable for an in-class essay assignment.

1. Choose some sport or leisure-time activity in which you participate or would like to participate, and write an essay about how it becomes an arena in which broad social issues are (or are not) addressed.

2. Because of Title IX and other laws, a great deal of information has been made public about matters like the relative funding for men's and women's athletic programs, support for women and men athletes, and grade-point ratios and graduation rates for participants in various sports. Do research on one of these topics or some related topic. An indispensable resource will be the *Chronicle of*

Higher Education's searchable database, which gives men's and women's participation rates, recruitment budget, coaching salaries, and other useful information for hundreds of schools. Find this database at <http://chronicle.com/stats/genderequity>. (If your college or university has an athletic program, you may wish to begin by seeking information about it.)

Such a broad topic offers several possibilities. Two examples with regard to this topic are (1) change across time and (2) differences within or across sports at one or several schools. You may decide to research a particular topic to get specific information ("What has this institution done with respect to Title IX?"). You may begin the research process with a particular question in mind ("Is the situation for men's college athletics in fact worse than it was five years ago?"). Or you may enter into this project with a specific agenda ("Colleges take unfair advantage of minority athletes"). Seek to make your arguments primarily arguments of fact and reason.

If several students in your class are working on this assignment, you may wish to coordinate your research so that combined, your papers will provide thorough information about a range of issues. This information can then be the basis for informed argument about possible future courses of action.

3. Are there limits to the extent to which corporations and businesses should be involved in leisure-time activities? What are these limits, and what determines (or should determine) them? Is it possible to balance, for example, the conflicting needs and wants of the involved parties—consumers (or spectators), participants, owners, and sponsors? Write an essay in which you explore these issues. Your essay will likely be most successful if you examine a single, specific leisure-time activity. You may wish to conduct research on a local event—a race that raises funds for a "good cause" or a cultural festival—and use it as the basis of your argument.

CHAPTER 24

What's It Like to Be Bilingual in the United States?

The readings in this chapter focus on issues relating to language, its varieties, and the way we decide when, where, and with whom to speak different languages. The readings remind us that issues of language and identity are all around us — in every conversation and every text. In all of these cases, language functions as a tool for communicating information about the world and as a symbol of who we — as speakers, signers, or writers — are or wish to be. Part of the meaning of any variety of language is its value in various linguistic "markets" — on the street, in communities where it is spoken, in communities where it isn't, in the classroom, on the basketball court, during prayers. The decision to use English or another language or variety is a complex decision that must take into account much more than which language one prefers.

If we take language as a prism through which to view identity (and hence society), we appreciate how challenging it is to negotiate common ground on which to construct our arguments about language. As these texts remind us, however, if thoughtful arguments about language are to take place, we have no choice but to struggle with these challenges. These texts also remind us of the need to engage in such arguments. In this regard, they show us that language is not different from many other sources of social difference in our society — or others.

Tom Meyer *Just 180 Days to Learn Miwok*   pp. 737–738

1. What is Tom Meyer's argument in this cartoon?

   We can't expect immigrant children to learn English in one school year because it is too difficult.

2. Can we state his argument without relating the history of California (and the United States) to current events? Why or why not?

Much of the cartoon's meaning is lost if readers don't understand that the 180 days refers to a situation in California's school system. Outside that connection, readers might still understand the cartoon's point about the hypocrisy of forcing immigrants to learn English when the colonizers of the Americas brought their own languages with them.

What does this fact tell us about Meyer's invoked audience? (For a discussion of invoked audience, see Chapter 1.)

Meyer's invoked readers are people who are aware of California's Proposition 227.

3. Many would claim that Meyer is using irony to make his argument. How does he accomplish this? (For a discussion of the use of irony and other tropes in argumentation, see Chapter 12.)

It is ironic that Europeans came to the Americas and forced their languages on the indigenous peoples and that Americans now continue to force their language on all who arrive in the United States, even though they never had to make a similar sacrifice. Had pilgrims and early colonists had to learn an indigenous language, they probably would have returned home to England.

4. Miwok is a severely endangered, even moribund, language. The remaining varieties of the language are spoken by only a few elders, although some younger Miwok are trying to learn and even revitalize the language. How might American history and the history of indigenous peoples in America be different if these groups had had the power to force European settlers to learn their languages? Why were the settlers not interested in doing so?

If indigenous groups in the Americas had had the power to insist that newcomers learn their languages, we might now have a wealth of different languages in the United States. Indigenous cultures might have been more prosperous and celebrated.

5. Although most of the indigenous languages of the United States have become extinct, not all have. Do some research on the language(s) of Native Americans who live in your home state or the state where you attend college or university. Write a summary of the information you find about the status and vitality of one or

more of these languages as if you were planning to post the summary in a public forum like Wikipedia. (If you're not familiar with Wikipedia, visit <http://wikipedia.com>.)

Answers will vary.

6. Writing assignment

Classroom Exercise: focus on the world

Ask students if they can imagine an America where the pilgrims and later colonists learned and used the languages of Native Americans. What might current U.S. culture look like had our history been different in that way? Students might be divided into groups to list points or describe how assimilating to indigenous languages might have affected the assimilation of other aspects of indigenous culture.

Janny Scott *Foreign Born in U.S. at*
             Record High   pp. 739–742

1. Like many news articles, Scott's argument is informative: her goal is to inform readers of the *Times* about the topic of immigration from several perspectives. Develop a list of the specific generalizations she makes and the sorts of evidence she cites for them. (For a discussion of what counts as evidence, see Chapter 16.) What consequences might these generalizations have for bi- or multilingualism in the United States? Why?

   One generalization she makes is that "foreign-born residents were much more likely than native Americans to live in and around a handful of big cities" (paragraph 3). She cites a Census Bureau study that notes that in states most heavily populated with foreign-born residents, the majority live in large metropolitan areas (paragraph 3).

2. A particularly interesting aspect of this article is its use of visual information in the two graphs in "Head Count." As you can see, one bar graph shows (for the past 110 years) the number of people in the United States born in another country or having at least one foreign-born parent, while the other shows the percentage of the total population each group represents for each ten-year cohort. What do we learn from each graph?

We learn from the number graph that there has been a great increase in the number of people born in this country to at least one foreign-born parent. We learn from the percentage graph that there has been a significant decrease in the percentage of those foreign-born or the offspring of those foreign-born in the total U.S. population.

From the two graphs together?

While there has been an increase in the number of people who were foreign-born or were the offspring of someone foreign-born, their overall percentage in the population has decreased.

Why is it important to consider both kinds of historical information in understanding immigration? In understanding bi- or multilingualism in the United States?

Looking at only one graph might encourage misunderstanding. Looking solely at the number graph, for example, might imply that with the increase in number came an increase in percentage. Looking solely at the percentage graph might imply that the decrease in percentage was sparked by a decrease in number. Each graph alone might encourage wrong conclusions.

3. As "Head Count" notes, the Census Bureau did not ask questions about the birthplace of parents in 1940, 1950, 1980, or 1990. What challenges does this fact present for students of immigration? Of American bi- or multilingualism?

Students of immigration would not be able to tell how many immigrants remained in the country and had children. Students of American bi- or multilingualism would not know how many bi- or multilingual respondents grew up speaking another language in the home because their parent was born in another country.

4. Writing assignment

Classroom Exercise: focus on the world

Conduct a study of your town—by finding census information on the numbers of people who were either born in another country or are the children of parents born in another country. If you can find information in several census reports, create graphs similar to those in the "Head Count" section of Scott's essay. How do your numbers compare with those that Scott cites? How do they differ? Why might your location have similar or different results? Consider the nature of your town and the criteria Scott cites for locations that attract those who are foreign-born.

Pew Hispanic Center/   *2002 National Survey*
Kaiser Family Foundation   *of Latinos*   pp. 743–751

1. What is your response to this information? Were you already aware of the situation described in the report, or did this selection present you with information or perspectives that were new? How? Why?

   Answers will vary.

2. This report from the Pew Hispanic Center/Kaiser Family Foundation represents an increasingly common genre of writing: the presentation of quantitative information in summary form so that it can be used by many sorts of researchers for many purposes. How have the creators of this report written it with the users in mind? In other words, what features of the text help readers with respect to understanding and using the data? How?

   The creators of the report take each set of data points from the graphs and summarize them verbally, offering both an observation of the data and an indication of the significance of those data.

3. What does this report teach us about language among Americans who identify as Latino or Hispanic? About bilingualism? About identity?

   Answers will vary, but students will likely note that individuals who identify as Latino and Hispanic have a wide variety of language experiences. No sweeping generalizations can be drawn about their ability and preferences with English or Spanish. In addition, bilingualism is quite common, although it exists in different balances of Spanish and English. Finally, many factors concerning language use and bilingualism affect individual and community identity.

4. Writing assignment

This study presents compelling research written in both graph form and summary form. Write an editorial for your local newspaper that makes an argument based on the data reported here. What would you choose as your claim? What elements of the report would you focus on? While this report offers a clear collection of arguments from facts and reason, you will likely want to include other lines of argument. Consider how you would use the data here to craft arguments from the heart, of character, and of values. Finally, consider your audience. How would they relate to the study here? How might that affect your writing choices?

Rolando Briseño *Bicultural Tablesetting*   pp. 752–753

1. The title of Rolando Briseño's painting, *Bicultural Tablesetting*, can be read as an argument of several sorts. In what ways might it be seen as an argument of definition?

   Briseño's painting uses symbols to define the Mexican and American sides of this bicultural experience. He is also defining biculturalness as being both divided down the middle and swirled together as on the plate.

   Of evaluation? (Which items in the painting are associated with Spanish-language or Mexican culture? Which are associated with English-language or American culture? Are these two groups of associations valued differently? By whom and why?)

   The evaluative argument is evident in the presence of the cell phone that belongs to the American side and represents modern modes of communication that lack the personal contact valued in Mexican culture.

2. How can we interpret Briseño's painting as an argument about tradition and innovation? About separation, segregation, and difference?

   The two sides of the table may represent Mexican and American cultures and may also make a statement about the modern life that America, with its cell phones, represents. The two different table patterns create a juxtaposition of the two cultures and a boundary between the two sides.

   About the nature of bilingual and bicultural life?

Bilingual and bicultural life can be conceptualized as a divided identity that does not match but at the same time that allows many people to develop a blended or mixed identity.

About *mestizaje*, the Spanish word used to refer to "cultural mixing," specifically the contact between Europeans and indigenous peoples in the Americas?

The plate of tomatoes in the middle of the plate creates a whir of mixing that involves both sides of the tablesetting. This blending of culture can be seen even as a mixing of heritage or blood.

3. In what ways might we see Briseño's painting as an argument from the heart? One based on Briseño's ethos? One based on facts or reason?

The tablecloths and table setting invite the audience to recall picnics or meals from their own family experiences. The detail in the painting leads one to believe that Briseño is a credible commentator. The details depict the two different cultures in various ways, as if presenting facts to be interpreted by the audience. In this sense, the argument is based on fact and reason.

4. Writing assignment

Classroom Exercise: focus on the argument

Ask students to reflect on multicultural aspects of their own lives. Are their parents immigrants? Are their parents each from different backgrounds? Are they the first in their families to go to college? Are they nontraditional students? If the answers to all of these are negative, then perhaps those students should consider what their "table setting" looks like now as a result of their own life experiences. Have students create a visual representation of identity in a table setting or some other image that that better suits them. The identities that each student chooses to portray need not be limited to race or ethnicity. How does expressing identity visually in this manner compare to writing an essay about the same topic?

Myriam Marquez *Why and When We Speak Spanish*
in Public pp. 754–755

1. How does Marquez explain and justify her behavior and that of many immigrants, including Spanish-speaking immigrants? What fear does she acknowledge on the part of those who don't speak Spanish? How does she seek to respond to it?

She explains that her respect for her parents and her country of origin has led her to speak Spanish in public. She acknowledges the fear that English is necessary to get ahead in the United States and the fear on the part of foreign-born parents that their children are becoming so "American" that they are abandoning their Spanish roots. She responds to these fears by sharing examples of how the United States has supported bi- and multilingualism from its inception.

2. What are the specific ways in which Marquez relies on arguments based on values, arguments from the heart, arguments based on character, and arguments based on reason to make her point? What values does Marquez appeal to when she explains why bilinguals like her speak Spanish in public?

She makes an argument based on values when she notes that "Being an American has very little to do with what language we use during our free time in a free country" (paragraph 7). She draws on the value of freedom in the United States and the value of respect for one's family and country to explain why bilinguals speak Spanish in public. Her discussion of the respect for family and country is also an argument from the heart, as it draws on the reader's own emotional connections with family and country. She makes an argument based on character by describing her own experiences as a bilingual speaker who chooses to speak Spanish in public. She makes an argument based on facts and reason when she notes that the U.S. government has never designated an official language.

3. The last three paragraphs of this essay represent a clear shift in tone and emphasis from the rest of this selection, especially the previous few paragraphs. What is their purpose?

Their purpose is to show that Marquez is not trying to exclude English speakers and that the respect she discusses earlier holds not only for her parents but for everyone she interacts with.

Do you find that they contribute to or detract from the overall effect of the selection? Why?

Answers will vary.

4. Writing assignment

Classroom Exercise: focus on the world

Have you ever been stuck in a conversation with a group of computer technicians? Or skateboarders? Or literary scholars? Or best friends? You might discover that while they're speaking English, they're using enough jargon, slang, or field-specific terminology to make their speech nearly unintelligible to an outsider. Consider the language choices you make with different groups of people. What words or phrases would you use around some people and not others? How does your speech change when you move among different groups? Choose a well-known fairy tale, and tell it as you would to your closest friends, your coworkers, people within your major, and some other group distinguished by language. Who are the included and excluded audiences from each retelling? What conclusions or connections can you draw between your retelling and Marquez's argument?

Sandra Cisneros From *Bien Pretty*   pp. 756–757

1. For Cisneros—and one can likely claim it for all bilinguals—the languages she knows aren't equal in some sense. Rather, each language is associated with different worlds of experience. What does Spanish connote for the narrator in Cisneros's text? What does English connote? Where would such connotations come from?

Spanish connotes memories from home and family life because it is the language she grew up with, the language spoken inside her home. English has harsh, stiff connotations, "starched *r*'s and *g*'s" (paragraph 5), likely because she grew up with it being used for official business, with those outside of her family and community.

2. Whereas Myriam Marquez writes about the use of Spanish in public, Cisneros writes about the use of Spanish in the most private of contexts. Are there things Marquez and Cisneros (or at least her narrator) would agree about? What might they be? Why?

Answers will vary, but students might note that both authors agree that speaking Spanish connects them with family, with their community, and with their origins.

3. One resource bilingual writers have is codeswitching: switching between the languages they know. In this excerpt, we see a simple noun phrase "la Alhambra" (paragraph 4) from Spanish, which we can correctly understand even if we know no Spanish. We also see the phrase "*Ya, ya, ya,*" (paragraph 9), which is followed immediately by the English equivalent, "There, there, there." Yet we also find the phrases "mi vida, mi preciosa, mi chiquitita" (paragraph 4), which we may not be able to figure out the meanings of. (In fact, the phrases translate literally as "my life, my precious [one], my dearest little [one]" — things native speakers of English wouldn't normally say to one another, even when being intimate. Such phrases are perfectly normal among speakers of Spanish.) Why might writers purposely create texts that include parts readers may not be able to understand? Why would such a strategy be especially effective when talking about intimacies like making love?

Writers might use codeswitching to mirror their normal speech patterns among bilingual friends and family. In addition, they might want to leave some elements of their story out of their reader's comprehension. For Cisneros, lovemaking remains a private act because her English-speaking readers cannot understand Flavio's sweet nothings.

4. Writing assignment

Classroom Exercise: focus on style

Using Chapter 12 (Style in Arguments) as a guide, analyze Cisneros's use of figurative language. How does she use literary tropes such as metaphors, similes, and analogies to make her writing more compelling? How does she use syntactic schemes for the same purpose? What sentences, phrases, paragraphs, or ideas do you find most striking? Why? How does her writing style affect your reading, understanding, analysis, and evaluation of her argument?

Marjorie Agosín *Always Living in Spanish*   pp. 758–760

Marjorie Agosín *English*   pp. 761–763

1. Why does Agosín write only in Spanish? How do her reasons for using Spanish compare with those of Marquez and Cisneros? How does she regard using Spanish as relating to her ancestry as a Jew?

   She writes only in Spanish to keep the memories of her childhood alive. She, Marquez, and Cisneros all see Spanish as connected with their family, with their community, and with their home. Growing up in a Jewish family that was forced to flee, Agosín sees language as a key to memory, often the only way to remember what you were forced to leave behind.

2. What sort of experiences did Agosín have while trying to learn English? How typical do you think her experiences were? In other words, how do Americans who are native speakers of English treat nonnative speakers of English? How did Spanish represent a source of strength and consolation to Agosín during the period when she was learning English?

   She was ridiculed and insulted, and she constantly felt the need to explain to English speakers why her English was so poor. She was treated as an outsider and given less respect than a native speaker of English was given. Spanish was a strength and consolation because it connected her with her identity, the world she left behind, the security of her family, and the space in which she belonged.

3. What does Spanish represent for Agosín? Why would it represent these things for her?

   Answers will vary but might include the notion that Spanish represents many of her memories from Chile — plants and flowers, family, friendship, warmth. It represents these things because it's connected to her memories of childhood and to her nostalgia for the country and family she left behind.

4. Writing assignment

How is Agosín's poem similar to and different from her essay? How does one text help you understand the other? What argument does each make? Do you think one is more effective than the other? Why? Why would the editors of this textbook choose to include both the essay and the poem?

Lan Cao *The Gift of Language*   pp. 764–770

1. What is your initial response to this excerpt from Cao's novel? Given the mother's cultural expectations, which she has brought from Vietnam, is it logical for her to respond as she does?

   Answers will vary.

   In what sense is Cao forced to parent her mother?

   She must teach her mother how to behave properly in the United States.

2. How does Cao construct the argument she makes here? What sorts of evidence does she rely on? How does she use language effectively to convey her ideas? (Chapters 6, 16, and 12, respectively, will help you answer these questions.)

   Cao uses specific incidents, such as their experience buying pork at the supermarket, to describe the process of immigrating and the effect it had on her relationship with her mother. She uses vivid descriptions of the two markets to note their extreme differences.

3. The tale that Cao tells has been told many times in the writings of immigrants, especially those who arrive in the United States as children with parents who speak little or no English. What are the consequences for family life? How does language become a source of power for the child? How does this power disrupt the traditional patterns of family life?

   Family dynamics shift. Children must grow up fast and be able to explain the ways of this new country to their parents, and parents must accept the authority of their children.

4. Writing assignment

Although this is an excerpt from a novel, Cao makes a clear argument here. Conduct a Toulmin analysis of Cao's argument. What is her claim? What are her reasons? What are her grounds to support her claim? What are her underlying warrants, and what backing does she provide for them? Does she provide any qualifiers and rebuttals? Do you think her argument is effective or ineffective? Why? How does the fact that this is an excerpt from a novel affect your analysis of the argument?

Andrea Lo *Finding Myself through Language* pp. 771–775

1. How does this essay recount Lo's changing understanding of her own identity and the roles that language and labels have played in it? In what ways has she let Chinese define her identity even as (or perhaps because) she struggled against it?

   Lo spent much of her childhood trying to establish an identity as "American" and not "Chinese," but she came to realize that she is a mix of the two, a "Chinese-American." She forced herself not to learn Mandarin and Cantonese and distanced herself from family and community, and yet she continued to be considered "Chinese" because of her appearance and her family.

2. What might Lo's comment in paragraph 2 that "'I'm American even though I look Chinese'" mean? After all, she was born in the United States. What does an American look like? What does it mean when Americans say, "You don't look American," to someone like Lo?

   Answers will vary but will likely note that her comment and the phrase "You don't look American" both refer to a stereotypical understanding that an "American" is racially Caucasian. Lo tries to distinguish between racial heritage and country of origin.

3. One memorable aspect of this essay is its use of crisp detail. Choose three specific examples of detail that Lo uses, explaining how each contributes to her point, both in the paragraph in which the detail occurs and in the essay overall.

   Answers will vary.

4. Writing assignment

Lo grapples with labels and their various implications. She wavers between different self-identifiers such as "Chinese-American" and "chinese-American." To the younger Lo, each seemed inadequate to describe herself. How would you describe yourself? If you had the power to construct a hyphenated identifier that highlighted the aspects you thought were most important for someone to understand who you were, what name would you choose? Would you name your ethnicity? Race? Gender? Sexuality? Hobbies? Major? Why do you choose the labels you do? How do you hope to be seen by those around you?

Mary Pipher *"Language"* and *"High School"* from *The Middle of Everywhere: Helping Refugees Enter the American Community* pp. 776–780

1. Pipher clearly believes that language presents a great challenge for refugees. How does she characterize the nature of this challenge? How persuasive is she? Why?

    Pipher characterizes the nature of the challenge of learning English as a situation of vulnerability and loss of control. She connects learning language to learning cultural norms. She creates an ethos of credibility by providing examples of different learners and describing a comparable situation for the reader to relate to.

2. In the excerpt on language, Pipher notes that "It takes most people from one to three years to learn social English and five to seven years to learn academic English" (paragraph 1), a claim that much research supports. How is this claim in conflict with movements like California's Proposition 227, discussed in the opening selection of this chapter, "Just 180 Days to Learn Miwok"?

    Proposition 227 offers immigrant children 180 days to learn English rather than one to three years.

    Why, in your opinion, might some Americans want to assume that schoolchildren coming from home where a language other than English is used can master English sufficiently within a school year?

    Answers will vary.

131

3. What challenges in particular do high-school-aged refugees face at school? As Pipher describes American high schools, only a small part of what occurs there involves the mastery of information learned in classes. What other developmental tasks are high-school-aged students engaging in? (Here, *developmental task* means any task related to growing up or to becoming an adult member of American culture.) Given the background and life experience of refugees, why are these tasks particularly difficult for them?

Many refugee children have trouble relating to people from other cultures and even interacting socially. Some children have been fleeing from war or mourning family members rather than learning age-appropriate social skills. Even after arriving in U.S. high schools, these students are inundated with other activities — like working, translating for family members, and recovering from traumatic experiences.

4. Writing assignment

Classroom Exercise: focus on rhetoric

How does Pipher use vignettes to strengthen her argument? What makes a first-person participant observation a better choice for supporting Pipher's claims than a report using statistics and historical points? In what situation would more formal evidence be more appropriate? Which type of evidence would be more likely to convince the government to continue or increase programs for refugees?

National Institute *"En la Comunidad Latina Tenemos*
of Mental Health *Una Cultura de Silencio"* pp. 781–782

1. The advertisement for the National Institute of Mental Health (NIMH) is primarily in Spanish. Why? How do language choice and targeted audience interact in this advertisement? Why might the designers have included the phrase "Real Men. Real Depression." in English?

This advertisement seems to target Hispanic men because mental health is a shameful topic in that community, espe-

cially among men. The choice of Spanish makes it clear even to bilingual men that the message is for them. "Real Men. Real Depression." may be the official motto of the campaign to reach men in all languages. The subtle codeswitching might also reach bilingual men.

2. Evaluate this advertisement as an argument. What roles does the personal testimony of Rodolfo Palma-Lulión play in the advertisement? Does it matter than Palma-Lulión is a university student? Why or why not? Are the design and layout of the advertisement effective and appropriate? Why or why not?

The testimony of Palma-Lulión allows the male audience to relate to him as another man. As a university student he represents someone who is educated and successful and yet struggles with depression. The shadowed face of the young man is appropriate because he is coming out of the darkness and showing his face, which works as a metaphor for the goals of NIMH.

3. Some Americans might criticize NIMH for producing advertisements or running programs in any language other than English. What arguments might they use for such criticisms? What costs might there be if NIMH does not produce advertisements or design programs in languages other than English?

The NIMH uses different languages to reach different audiences that need their help. Not addressing audiences that do not speak English would leave a large section of the population without services and could mean that more emergency services would be required in the future.

4. Writing assignment

Classroom Exercise: focus on the world

Some argue that American advertisements and public-service announcements should be presented in English and that presenting them in other languages enables people to avoid learning English. Why would NIMH create a Spanish-language campaign? Why might a business make advertisements in other languages? Does this sound like a good business practice? How would you react to people from Miami or Los Angeles who felt that Spanish advertising was invading their cityscape?

Samuel G. Freedman *It's Latino Parents Speaking*
Out on Bilingual Education
Failures pp. 783–786

1. As in most newspapers arguments, and especially columns that comment on contemporary issues while including quotations from various parties, this article includes several simultaneous arguments. What argument(s) are the Latino parents from Mexico and the Dominican Republic making?

   Parents are afraid that their children will not learn English well enough if they stay in bilingual classrooms.

   What argument is the mayor's office making?

   The mayor's office is also against bilingual education in favor of full-immersion classrooms.

   What argument is the Industrial Areas Foundation making?

   Without stating their claims specifically, the foundation seems to concur with the mayor's office, expressing doubt about current bilingual programs that teachers and administrators are defending.

   Finally, what argument is Freedman making?

   Freedman argues that children in bilingual education may never enter the mainstream and that the current bilingual system is merely a niche for bilingual teachers and bureaucrats.

2. As Freedman notes, bilingual education remains a very controversial topic in New York City. Why do recent Latino immigrants — Mexicans and Dominicans — oppose the idea of bilingual education? Freedman also refers to a lawsuit filed by the Puerto Rican Legal Defense Fund, which dates from 1973, that mandated bilingual education in New York City. In this case, *Aspira vs. Board of Education of the City of New York*, Aspira, a group of middle-class Puerto Rican professionals, successfully filed suit against the city's Board of Education, arguing that the school board's programs did not meet the needs of Puerto Rican students, especially those who did not speak English well. Why might Puerto Ricans, in particular, have been and remain supportive of bilingual education? (Freedman doesn't discuss this issue. If you don't know the answer, you'll

need to do some research to get information about the linguistic situation on Puerto Rico, a self-governing commonwealth of the United States. Although Puerto Ricans are U.S. citizens, they can't vote in federal elections, nor do they pay taxes.)

Recent immigrants might be more interested in having their children learn English, and Puerto Ricans in New York might be more interested in preserving their island culture and language. Puerto Ricans, as U.S. citizens, might also see Spanish education as something that they could expect at home and thus as a right that travels with them.

3. How does Freedman use the trope of irony in this article, especially in its ending? (For a discussion of irony, see Chapter 12.)

It might seem ironic that immigrant parents want their children mainstreamed rather than put into special classes aimed at nonnative speakers. Another irony is that parents who wanted their children to learn English accidentally put their children in bilingual classes by signing a waiver that they did not understand.

4. Writing assignment

Classroom Exercise: focus on the argument

What is bilingual education? Are there different kinds of bilingual education? Should different communities of parents have a say in the type of bilingual education that is offered to their children? If you were a school board member who was presented with Freedman's article, what other information would you want before making any policy decisions? What other people or specialists would you want to interview?

Firoozeh Dumas From *Funny in Farsi: A Memoir of Growing Up Iranian in America* pp. 787–791

1. How might we summarize Firoozeh Dumas's argument in this essay? What is its exact subject — the importance of names, the ways in which Americans have traditionally responded to unfamiliar names, the immigrant experience, all of these?

Dumas's argument is that a name is an integral part of human identity. The subject of the article revolves around how Americans respond to names and what they assume from names. This look at names is interesting because an immigrant's point of view is presented.

2. Carefully reread paragraph 12 of the essay, in which Dumas explains how having an "American" name and speaking English without a foreign accent was like having "X-ray glasses." Is Dumas's portrayal of Americans in this passage and in the essay more broadly flattering? Humorous? Honest? In this passage, Dumas notes that "people assumed I was American." What definition of "American" must she (and those about whom she writes) be assuming?

   Dumas talks about certain people's responses to her when assuming she was American. These people and those that avoid pronouncing foreign names (Americans) are not portrayed in a positive light. "American" is conversely broadened to apparently mean someone born in the United States who speaks English without an accent.

   Is such a definition valid, given evidence she presents elsewhere in the essay and the fact that the United States likes to think of itself as a nation of immigrants? At what point does an immigrant become an American?

   Answers will vary.

3. How would you describe Dumas's use of humor in this essay? Find three examples that you especially like, and explain how the humor helps the author achieve her goals. In what ways does Dumas's argument represent satire, with the simultaneous goals of ridiculing and remedying a problematic situation? (For a discussion of uses of humor, including satire, in argumentation, see Chapter 13.)

   Answers will vary.

4. How does Dumas use the repeated metaphor of the spice cabinet to help structure her argument? Why is this metaphor an appropriate one, given her topic? How does this metaphor permit her to critique the mother who called her "F Word" (paragraph 17)?

The metaphor of spice can be used to talk about the sounds of language, cultural experiences, comforts, and the willingness to try new things. This usage is particularly appropriate for her topic and allows her to accuse the mother from her children's school of refusing to add to her spice cabinet.

5. Writing assignment

Classroom Exercise: focus on the world

Have students ever chosen a new name in a language class? How did they feel about that? Have they ever traveled to a foreign country and changed the pronunciation of their name or chosen a whole new name to make other people feel more comfortable? To fit in better? Have they chosen to keep their own name even when the pronunciation is very different from the host language? Was it frustrating to hear their name presented so differently? What is it about our names that holds so much personal identity and meaning when it is just a word?

Wrap-up Exercises for Constructing Arguments about Being Bilingual in the United States

These assignments are suggested as wrap-up exercises in which students can integrate any or all of the readings of the chapter. Either would be suitable for an in-class essay assignment.

1. Write an essay in which you take to task the writer whose argument you find least convincing among those you read in this chapter. In other words, critique that writer's argument, demonstrating why your perspective on the topic is better supported. One of your tasks as a writer will be to summarize the argument you're critiquing so that readers unfamiliar with the original text will understand both the original writer's position and yours.

2 Write an argument about language(s) and identities in which you incorporate your own experiences as a user of the language varieties you know (or those you do not know). How, for example, do you imagine your life might be different if you knew certain languages or certain varieties of English, or how would it be different if you did not know the language(s) or varieties that you do? How would the command of these linguistic varieties shape

your identity as an individual or as a member of the groups to which you belong?

Another way of imagining this assignment, if you are monolingual, is to think about what your life would have been like if you'd grown up in a community where a language other than English was used (perhaps exclusively, perhaps in addition to English). What challenges might you have faced thus far with respect to mastering the language(s) of your home community? Those used outside the home community? How might dealing with these challenges have influenced the way you perceive yourself both inside and outside the community? Similarly, if you grew up bilingually, imagine what your life would be like if you were monolingual. How would you be different?

CHAPTER 25

What Does Your Language Say about Your Identity?

The connection between language and identity is far more complex than just bilingualism. Every aspect of how we choose to express ourselves in language—word choices, intonation, style, delivery—sends a message about who we are and how we identify ourselves. All of us have choices we can make about language. Amy Tan writes of her desire to use all of her Englishes, but she knows that those choices and the consequences of making them are constrained in significant ways. Each variety earns respect in one "market" but is "dissed" in others. The choices that we make are reflections of ourselves.

Thinking about language in these ways raises complex questions of ownership. Does Standard English belong to everyone or only to people from a certain class and ethnic background, as David Troutt contends? If he's correct, would we be distressed? Should we try to change the situation? Can white hip-hoppers claim to use Ebonics? How will such claims be evaluated by African American hip-hoppers? By African Americans at large? By the majority society?

Such questions remind us that human beings have far more invested in language and languages than we generally realize. After all, it is one of the major resources from which we fashion who we are. It is not surprising, then, that language varieties come to stand in for other, more volatile varieties of difference. It's no longer legal to refuse to hire someone because of his or her ethnicity, but it's still perfectly legal to refuse to hire someone because of the degree of his or her accent or the linguistic varieties he or she has or hasn't mastered. Further, mastery of certain aspects of Standard English continues to serve as prerequisite for academic success. Similarly, because it's impossible for Americans, at least, to think about language varieties without moving into discussions of correctness—what is right and what is wrong—we should not be surprised to find that linguistic varieties can be associated with certain moral or ethical values. People who speak one way or another are labeled "hard working," whereas those who speak another way are labeled "lazy." In short, ways of using language are intimately linked with matters of power and group membership.

Chicago Women's Club   *Pledge for Children*   pp. 795–796

Note: The authors found the text of this pledge on pp. 155–156 of Dennis Baron's *The English-Only Question: An Official Language for Americans?* (New Haven: Yale UP, 1990).

1. What sorts of arguments are being made by this pledge? In other words, how is Americanness defined in general?

   Americanness involves honor, pleasantness, gentleness, sincerity, and love of learning.

   With respect to language use in particular?

   Americans use clear, well-modulated, sincere, and carefully articulated speech.

   According to the pledge, how does the "ideal American," or the American who loves his or her country, speak?

   The ideal American speaks without any audible trace of a language other than schoolbook English.

2. According to the criteria of the pledge, do you qualify as an "ideal American"? Does that trouble you in any way? Why or why not? How do you think you'd respond if you'd been given such a pledge as, say, an eighth-grader? Why?

   Answers will vary.

3. Consider the table on p. 796, which presents statistics about immigrants in Chicago in 1900, 1910, 1920, and 1990. At the time the pledge was issued, many of the immigrants living in Chicago had come from Germany, Austria, Poland, and Russia and, to a far lesser extent, Ireland, Sweden, and Italy. Upon arrival, they were generally poor and uneducated. How do these figures, along with the 1918 pledge, construct an argument?

   They combine as two types of evidence—the pledge as an argument of values and the statistics as an inartistic argument from fact and reason.

What, specifically, is the argument?

The argument of the pledge and the statistics is that in Chicago there were enormous numbers of immigrants, that a huge percentage of children were being raised in immigrant homes, that English was perceived (by the Chicago Women's Club at least) as the "country's language," and that language was seen as an important tool for absorbing and integrating immigrants and their children into Americanness.

4. You're certainly aware that immigration and immigrants continue to be hot topics in American public discourse, the subject of much debate. Does language become part of these debates? If so, how? For example, do people comment on the presence of other languages in pubic space (as discussed by Myriam Marquez, "Why and When We Speak Spanish in Public (p. 754), bilingual media or media in languages other than English, or the way English is spoken by immigrants or their descendants? What specific forms do these comments take? What do they tell us about language and identity among some Americans?

Language will always be a part of any immigration debate. All of the examples given in the question above make clear that language plays a centrol role in public and in private, in schools, the workplace, and in the society at large. These comments take many different forms and may be articulated through a variety of texts, from the opinion page of the local newspaper, to school policies (school districts might or might not have provisions for second language learners), to electoral rights (some districts require voters to be accommodated in multiple languages). What this tells us is that language and identity are inseparable and intrinsically political.

5. Writing assignment

Classroom Exercise: focus on the world

Discuss in small groups one or more of the following questions: Can you imagine any organizations advocating the use of this pledge in U.S. elementary schools today? What organizations would they be? Would they want or need to change the pledge? How? Why? To what extent is the pledge specifically about the English language and to what extent about ways of speaking or behaving in general? Do you think such a pledge would be a good thing to give schoolchildren today? Why or why not?

Ariel Dorfman *If Only We All Spoke*
Two Languages   pp. 797–799

1. What event motivated Dorfman to write this essay?

He wrote it after the passage of the California referendum on bilingual education in 1998.

What seems to be his ultimate argument: that the United States should be multilingual (or encourage multilingualism), that it should be bilingual (or encourage bilingualism), or that it should become bilingual in English and Spanish (or encourage such bilingualism)? What evidence can you provide for your position?

He asserts that the United States should become multilingual, "with everyone here speaking at least two languages" (paragraph 1). It could also be argued, because of the ending line, that he advocates Spanish/English bilingualism specifically.

2. What experiences led to Dorfman's bilingualism?

He moved with his family from Argentina to New York at age two-and-a-half and soon after that spent three weeks in an isolation ward in a hospital where he was spoken to only in English. As an adolescent, he and his family moved to Chile.

How are his experiences similar to or different from those of the typical immigrant to the United States?

Like many children of immigrants, he put tremendous effort into being a "xenophobic all-American kid," distancing himself from his immigrant background and his first language. A notable difference is that his family moved once again, returning to a Spanish-speaking country where Dorfman had to resume using his native language. In addition, Dorfman attended private schools.

Why is this question in particular important when thinking about generalizing Dorfman's experiences to other situations?

Answers will vary.

3. Supporters of the California referendum on bilingual education would likely argue that immigrants are free to speak, use, and pass on to their children any languages other than English that they might speak, but that they should not expect publicly funded schools to teach their children these languages. Does Dorfman anticipate or respond in any way to this criticism? If he does not, why not?

   He addresses it indirectly by mentioning the benefits of multilingualism to the nation as a whole (by having a populace with "an economic and political edge," paragraph 13). He might not address that criticism directly because he has chosen to speak more abstractly about the benefits of bilingualism or multilingualism.

   Can an argument that does not address the concerns of those taking an opposing view still be effective? Give reasons for your answer.

   Answers will vary.

4. Writing assignment

Classroom Exercise: focus on the argument

Dorfman's essay contains elements of three argument types — evaluation (bilingual education is good), causal ("the American experience and idiom are fertilized and fortified" by bilingualism), and proposal (the United States should embrace multilingualism as a good policy and goal). In addition, Dorfman uses three lines of argument — heart (his personal history), values (his appeal to patriotism and Americanness), and character (his credentials as an accomplished author in two languages). Ask students to analyze Dorfman's essay to find and identify the three types and the three lines. If time permits, discuss how each one contributes to the whole of Dorfman's argument, or think of how he might have worked in the fourth argument type, definition, and the fourth line of argument, fact and reason.

Chang-rae Lee *Mute in an English-Only World* pp. 800–803

1. Throughout the piece, Lee offers numerous insights into the strate-gies those who do not speak English well use to negotiate American society. List some of these strategies along with their consequences for people like Lee's mother and their loved ones.

   Answers will vary, but likely possibilities include relying on bilingual children to help interpret business transactions in the world or shopping in self-service stores where little or no speaking is required.

2. One of the interesting things about this essay from a rhetorical per-spective is the way in which Lee bucks reader expectations. Many readers would assume that the son of an immigrant, writing about his mother's struggles with English, would oppose a law mandat-ing the use of English in signs. How and why does Lee challenge reader expectations?

   Answers will vary.

   How does this use of his mother's experiences contribute to his ethos and authority?

   It lets readers know that he deeply understands the prob-lems and issues involved.

3. Writing assignment

4. Writing assignment

Classroom Exercise: focus on the argument

Lee deftly moves between present and past in his essay, including shifts between general description and narration of specific experi-ences. There are six time frames in the essay (paragraphs 1–2, 3–8, 9–15, 16, 17, 18–19). Find them, and examine his techniques for shift-ing time. Are they effective? Why or why not?

Amy Tan *Mother Tongue* pp. 804–809

1. How have Tan's attitudes toward her mother's English changed over the years? Why?

   She has learned that her mother's English is not "broken," and she is no longer ashamed. She understands that lan-

guage-learner grammar or accent did not diminish the quality of her mother's thoughts.

Have you had similar experiences with your parents or other older relatives?

Answers will vary.

2. Why, ultimately, is Tan suspicious of language ability tests? What are her complaints?

   She is suspicious of these tests because they can't measure richness of language use or of language perception. She is uncomfortable because the test questions have only one correct answer, as though they are math questions.

   What sorts of evidence does she offer?

   She uses an extended example of the limitations of analogy questions. These questions aim at only one specific relationship between two words even though there may be others. The person who perceives that richness is penalized.

   Do you agree or disagree with her argument? Why?

   Answers will vary.

3. Tan's text was written to be read aloud by the author herself. In what ways might this fact be important? (For a discussion of the features of spoken arguments, see Chapter 15.)

   Spoken texts require more and different signposts to help listeners keep track of the structure. They usually use simple sentences. Informal language is usually more acceptable in spoken texts.

   What would it be like, for example, to have heard Tan deliver this text? How would such an experience have been different from reading it on the page? Had Tan written the piece to be read silently by strangers—as her novels are, for example—how might she have altered it? Why?

   Answers will vary.

4. Writing assignment

Amy Tan and Chang-Rae Lee (author of the previous article, "Mute in an English-Only World") both write about their mothers and their mothers' language. Compare and contrast the ways in which these writers use their mothers' language and experiences with language as part of their argument.

John Rickford   *Suite for Ebony* and *Phonics*   pp. 810–817

1. In light of Rickford's argument, what do the following sentences from p. 814 mean: "Media uproar over Ebonics missed the point. What's really important is not what kind of language Ebonics isn't, but what kind it is"?

   Rickford argues that the goal of acquiring Standard English can be met more easily by acknowledging the validity of Ebonics as a linguistic system and using it as an explicit point of departure or comparison. He cites evidence showing the effectiveness of such a system.

2. What are the three theories of the origins of Ebonics that Rickford discusses?

   The theories are: (1) the Afrocentric theory (paragraphs 15–17); (2) the Eurocentric, or dialectologist, theory (paragraph 18); and (3) the creolist theory (paragraph 19).

   How effectively does he summarize each theory? (In other words, how clear an idea do you have of what each theory argues?)

   Answers will vary.

   What does he say are the strengths and weaknesses of each?

   The Afrocentric view accounts for some grammatical forms like verb tenses, but it doesn't account for some of the changes in pronunciation of consonant clusters. The Eurocentric view accounts for changes in consonant clusters but relies on there having been cultural exposure and contact that likely didn't actually occur. The principal strength of the creolist view is that it combines the strengths of the other two; its weakness may lie in its unprovability.

How persuasive is he in arguing for the creolist view, given the evidence he offers? Do you think Rickford assumes you will agree with him? Why or why not?

Answers will vary.

3. As Rickford notes, linguists contend that they study language scientifically. Assuming they do, how much knowledge about language or linguistics do you find in the other pieces about Ebonics in this cluster? What, in your opinion, accounts for the fact that the knowledge claimed by linguists, as scientists, is generally absent from public debates about language?

Answers will vary.

4. Writing assignment

Classroom Exercise: focus on the world

This exercise reinforces Rickford's explanation of the "rules" of pronouncing English that speakers obey unconsciously (paragraphs 9–10) and gives students an opportunity to practice with a probably unfamiliar concept. Consider the pronunciation of past-tense regular verbs. Although we spell them with -*ed*, we pronounce some, such as *saved*, with a *d* sound at the end and some, such as *soaked*, with a *t* sound at the end. Let students suggest other verbs with which to test the rule. Note that verbs with irregular past forms, such as *eat/ate* or *think/thought,* fall outside this pattern and that verbs ending in a *t* or *d* sound, such as *wait* or *wade*, require an additional syllable for the past form. Introduce a few invented nonsense verbs just to prove that we haven't all memorized all the forms by rote—*deeb, fup, luss, luzz*.

David D. Troutt   *Defining Who We Are
in Society*   pp. 818–821

1. Troutt begins with the assertion that "[p]erhaps nothing defines us more than our linguistic skills" (paragraph 2). Throughout the rest of the essay, what evidence does he offer for such a strong assertion?

". . . we treat our fluency like property." (paragraph 3)

"[Ebonics] then qualifies as a reliable measurement of the gulf between many poor blacks and the middle-class world where standard English is spoken." (paragraph 11)

"[Formally educated blacks] . . . may be ostracized for 'talking white.'" (paragraph 13)

All of paragraph 15

2. According to Troutt, how did the responses of Blacks and Whites to the Ebonics controversy differ?

"For many whites, it measures the contradictions of color-blind convictions. For many blacks, Ebonics measures the complications of assimilation and the resiliency of shame." (paragraph 6)

What were the origins and consequences of these differences?

"Many whites have used the issue as an opportunity to vent racist jokes ordinarily kept underground or in sports bars. . . . Others invoke it in order to restrict black cultural influences." (paragraph 7)

Again, what sorts of evidence does Troutt offer to support his position?

He mentions talk radio.

How, specifically, does he use the example of Jesse Jackson to demonstrate the ambivalence of most African Americans toward Ebonics?

Troutt mentions Jackson's original stance opposing the Oakland resolution and his subsequent change of mind (paragraph 14).

3. Writing assignment

Classroom Exercise: focus on the world

This exercise would be a good springboard for the writing assignment in Exercise 3 above. In small groups or together, ask students to discuss the following questions: Does Standard English belong to everyone? To what extent is it linked implicitly or explicitly to issues of class and ethnicity? To issues of gender or region?

Making a Visual Argument: Public Service Campaigns Use Language to Send a Message

National Youth Anti-Drug Media Campaign   *He Might Dump Me . . .; You Smoked Weed . . .; Labeled . . .; You Scan Me . . .; Filed under Pothead . . .*

pp. 822–827

1. Obviously, each of these advertisements is meant to discourage the use of illegal drugs. However, they represent different ways of doing so. In the lower right-hand corner of each advertisement, you'll find three different labels: "courage: the anti-drug," "regret: the anti-drug," and "i am my anti-drug." What sorts of appeals is each of these categories of ad making? How are those appeals linked to the content of each of the visual arguments—its subject, its image, and its text?

   All of the appeals are emotional in that they challenge the reader to imagine that they are the characters and situations in the photos. The courage label invites the audience to use logic over emotion in choosing to help someone who has a drug problem, and the regret label also speaks to an argument of fact in presenting the consequences of using drugs. The label "I am" presents an argument of character, with each character offering evidence of his or her achievements.

2. In what ways is the advertisement in the "courage: the anti-drug" campaign a proposal argument? In what way(s) are all of these advertisements proposal arguments? (For a discussion of proposal arguments, see Chapter 11.)

   The courage argument proposes that it is worth upsetting a loved one to help him or her get away from drugs. All of the advertisements propose that young people stay away from drugs.

3. In what ways are the advertisement in the "regret: the anti-drug" campaign a causal argument? In what way(s) are all of these advertisements causal arguments? (For a discussion of causal arguments, see Chapter 10.)

The regret argument posits that drug use can cause pain and regret for the user and the people that they hurt or disappoint. All of the advertisements argue that drugs keep people from realizing their dreams and being successful.

4. Who are the multiple audiences for the "i am my anti-drug" campaign? Whom are the advertisements addressing directly? Who are the invoked audiences?

   The first two advertisements directly address people who are involved with drugs—either because they use drugs or because a loved one does. The "I am" campaign invokes older people who do not use drugs. All of the pieces address people who are involved in drugs and serve as warnings for those who have not yet been in contact with drugs.

   Compare and contrast the three ads in this series. Which is most effective? Why? Do you contend this sort of argument in general is effective with the target audience? Why or why not?

   Answers will vary.

5. Writing assignment

Classroom Exercise: focus on the argument

Nancy Reagan's "Just Say No" campaign against drugs has become a staple of 80's Americana, but it is most often the subject of ridicule. What do students think about the "I am" campaign? Do they find it interesting? Modern? Timely? Informed? What makes an anti-drug campaign successful? Have students in pairs or groups design an ad that would complement the ones in this selection, or create a totally different one if they would like. Share the results with the class and discuss the characteristics that make the good ones notable.

Steve Rushin   *Hip Unchecked: In Sports and on TV,*
                   Sarcasm and Cynicism Are Drowning
                   Out Sincerity and Compassion   pp. 828–829

1. How well does the article's subtitle—"In Sports and on TV, Sarcasm and Cynicism Are Drowning Out Sincerity and Compassion"— summarize Rushin's argument?

   The subtitle summarizes Rushin's argument quite well, although he doesn't restrict his observation only to sports and TV. He claims sarcasm and cynicism are everywhere.

Why do you think that Rushin doesn't include an explicit thesis in his essay? How might doing so have altered the tone of the piece?

Doing so might have blunted his "wise guy" edge.

2. How would you describe the tone of Rushin's essay?

The tone is abrupt and smart-alecky but not antagonistic toward the audience.

To what extent does his tone enact the very attitudes and behaviors he's criticizing?

It does so to a large extent.

Do you think the tone contributes to or detracts from his argument? Why or why not?

Answers will vary.

3. Nearly all of Rushin's examples involve males. Is the pattern of behavior Rushin describes and criticizes "a guy thing" or "an American thing"? Why?

Answers will vary.

4. Writing assignment

Classroom Exercise: focus on the argument

What kind of argument is Rushin's article? Proposal? Causal? Evaluation? Some combination of those? What lines of argument does he use? Arguments from facts and reason? From character? Something else? A combination? Working in small groups, make an analysis of Rushin's argument according to its type(s) and line(s) of argument. Compare your group's conclusions with those of the other groups.

Deborah Tannen From *You're Wearing That?* pp. 830–836

1. How would you summarize Tannen's account of why mother/daughter communication is necessarily difficult?

Tannen discusses the messages and metamessages that pass between mothers and daughters.

Do you agree? Why or why not? Is mother/son communication less complex? Why or why not?

Answers will vary.

2. In the section "'You're Not Going to Wear That, Are You?'" Tannen distinguishes between the notions of *message* and *metamessage* (paragraph 20) and then continues by distinguishing between focusing on the message itself and "crying literal meaning" (paragraph 21), and focusing on the metamessage and the history of past conversations. In what ways is this section of her chapter a definitional argument? (For a discussion of definitional arguments, see Chapter 8.) Why is it important to the remainder of her analysis?

By defining *message* and *metamessage*, Tannen is able to pinpoint the aspect of the communication that is causing the problem. The author goes on to describe that often what women appreciate from each other is a metamessage of caring, support, and even approval.

3. Although Tannen's focus in this book is mother/daughter communication, this excerpt includes another of her favorite topics — male and female interactional styles. How does she characterize prototypical female and male interactional styles in the section "Who Cares?" Why is the notion of metamessage crucial in understanding such a characterization?

In "Who Cares?" Tannen points out that mother's and father's reactions to their daughter can be very different. Having a discussion rather than just engaging in problem solving can send a metamessage of caring to the daughter.

To what extent do you agree with her assessment of mothers' and fathers' (and hence female and male) ways of showing concern or interacting? Why?

Answers will vary.

4. What sorts of evidence does Tannen use to support her claims? (For a discussion of what counts as evidence, see Chapter 16.) Given that her goal is to understand and explicate the nature of interaction, how appropriate are the kinds of evidence she uses? What is the likelihood that other kinds of evidence would have been effective?

For evidence, Tannen uses actual conversations as reported by women whom she has interviewed. By dissecting the details of a conversation and the possible meanings behind

the messages, she is able to draw conclusions about the nature of communication. Because the topic is conversational
norms, the interview evidence is much more useful than
statistics about how mothers talk to daughters.

5. Writing assignment

Classroom Exercise: focus on rhetoric

Does Tannen's analysis ring true to students? Do they have similar accounts of misunderstandings and arguments with their mothers? At
what age did this relationship begin? What about men in the class—did
their relationship with their father become more complicated at a certain age? Is it a similar age to when women pinpoint a change in
relationships with their mothers? Have any students grown up in nontraditional families? If so, what can they add based on their experiences
with their guardians or caregivers? Do students see themselves eventu-
ally taking the parental role with their own grown-up children? What
suggestions do they have for avoiding upsetting their own children?

Making a Visual Argument: Gendering Language: Women and Men Speaking in *New Yorker* Cartoons

Mick Stevens   *Talk to Me Alice, I Speak Woman*

Leo Cullum   *The Emergence of Language*

William Hamilton   *Look, All I'm Saying Is . . .*

Roz Chast   An Excerpt from *Men Are from Belgium,
                 Woman Are from New Brunswick*

Pete Steiner   *And Do You, Deborah Tannen, Think They
                    Know What They're Talking About?*

pp. 837–840

1. What differences and similarities do you find among these cartoon-
   ists with respect to the way they represent the problems women
   and men often have in communicating? What different behaviors
   do men and women appear to engage in, based on these cartoons?

   **All of the cartoons suggest that women communicate dif-
   ferently than men do and that men have something to be
   afraid of in this difference. Some of the cartoons focus on**

153

language itself, while others comment on what women have to say and even how they problem solve.

2. With the exception of the cartoon by William Hamilton, "Look, all I'm saying . . . ," the cartoons all focus on heterosexual couples in interaction. What are the advantages and disadvantages of taking (adult) heterosexual couples as the best or only example of how men and women talk or interact?

   Comparing men and women in a couple relationship highlights differences in communication, but looking only at heterosexual couples focuses on communication that might be confounded by gender roles or by traditional relationship roles.

3. Which cartoon do you find most successful? Why? Which do you find least successful? Why?

   Answers will vary.

4. Much humor, especially in cartoons, depends on intertextuality — that is, shared references to other texts or, by extension, other things, like cultures or events, that can be "read" as texts. How does intertextuality play an important role in the cartoons by Roz Chast and Peter Steiner? (By the way, why do you suppose John Gray chose the title that he did for his book about communication between members of a heterosexual couple?)

   Our culture has many stereotypes about communication between women and men. Keeping those stereotypes in mind is necessary for finding the humor in the cartoons.

5. Using these cartoons as evidence, describe the kinds of people who are the intended audience of the *New Yorker*. What are their lives like? What values do they hold? What concerns do they have? What sorts of things are they expected to know about?

   The intended audience of the *New Yorker* seems to be educated, upper-middle-class people who are engaged in heterosexual relationships. These people read some academic literature, work in white-collar office jobs, and have some experience with psychotherapy. The readership is concerned about maintaining their relationships at home and at work. Readers are expected to be familiar with the work of Deborah Tannen and John Gray with gender stereotypes

about male and female communication styles, and with stereotypical attitudes about asking for directions.

6. Writing assignment

Classroom Exercise: focus on rhetoric

Have students discuss what they see as the major points of miscommunication between men and women. Then have each student design a cartoon that addresses one of these points. Students can share their work and discuss how visual arguments and texts work together or separately to present the message.

Wrap-up Exercises for Constructing Arguments about Language(s) and Identities

These two assignments are suggested as wrap-up exercises in which students can integrate any or all of the readings of the chapter. In addition, Exercise 1 would be suitable for an in-class essay assignment.

1. Write an essay in which you describe how the arguments in this chapter have challenged your ways of thinking about language and identities. In other words, what did you learn about language and its links to identity from the readings in this chapter? You might consider things that surprised you, opinions or arguments that made you angry, or issues you'd never considered in a systematic way before. If you contend that these readings have had no influence on the attitudes you hold toward language and identities, you should explain why not.

2. Choose an issue related to languages and identities not discussed in this chapter, and write an essay in which you take a stance on it. Topics are legion. For example: Should the Catholic Church return to the use of Latin in the Mass, as some contend? Should writers use gender-neutral language (for example, *he or she* instead of *he* and *firefighter* instead of *fireman*)? Should studying a foreign language be a requirement in high school or college? Should prime-time television shows permit the use of profanity? If so, which words? Recalling the distinction between an opinion and an informed opinion, you'll most assuredly need to do some research before constructing your argument.

CHAPTER 26

What Role Should Religion Play in Public Life?

Arguing about beliefs and stances invites us to consider both the positions that others take (and by contrast, the positions we might hold) and also the ways in which arguments about values are constructed. In doing so, the practice of argument prompts us to reflect on how people construct themselves as individuals and as members of a larger society. If you've ever spent time in another country, even another English-speaking one, you'll realize that different countries define the notion of "individual" and "member of our society" in different ways. One of the ways in which they do so is through arguing about religious beliefs and ideologies. The arguments that can be made and the stances that can be claimed ultimately define the nature of a society and the nature of an individual within it.

For these reasons, arguing about religious beliefs provides the occasion for us to examine who we are, who we aren't, and who we aspire to be. Such reflection ultimately forces us to ask difficult questions about argument in the United States:

- Is it possible to argue publicly about fiercely held beliefs in a pluralistic society? Must such arguments end up as shouting matches, or are there alternatives? When, if ever, are shouting matches warranted? When, if ever, might alternatives prove useful? Should the goal of arguments about beliefs be winning or something else? Why?
- Is freedom of religion in the United States little more than freedom from religious discourse, at least as far as the public arena is concerned? Are there ways to permit people of faith to honor their beliefs while respecting the rights of others (either those of other faiths or those who claim no faith at all), or should public discourse seek to avoid any mention of faith?

- Are there only two sides to every argument? What is gained or lost if we acknowledge that reality is always more complex than any dichotomies we might propose?

Laurie Goodstein *More Religion, but Not the Old-Time Kind* pp. 844–850

1. How would you characterize Laurie Goodstein's argument in this selection?

   Goodstein's argument is that there is currently a surge in religious activity around the world but that it does not have the trappings of fundamentalism that were present in the past.

   Why might it be important to contextualize her subject — religion as a "rising force" — globally?

   Understanding the influence of religion globally means taking into account many different religious and political situations all over the world.

   How would you characterize the ethos Goodstein creates in discussing this topic? Why might she do so? (For a discussion of how writers create their ethos and why it's important, see Chapter 3.)

   Answers will vary.

2. Like many complex arguments, this selection contains arguments of several kinds, including definitional arguments. Based on the information given in this selection, how would you define and distinguish among the categories "fundamentalists," "evangelicals," and "Pentecostals?"

   Goodstein characterizes fundamentalists as focusing on doctrine and inerrancy. She states that evangelicals participate in revival meetings and attend seminaries, but she does not give a clear picture of evangelicals. She describes Pentecostals as putting much importance on "spirit-filled worship," speaking in tongues, and miracle healings.

   Are these definitions adequate for this context—that is, for understanding the information presented in this selection? Why or why not? (For a discussion of definitional arguments, see Chapter 8.)

   Answers will vary.

3. This selection also offers a number of causal claims. List three. What sorts of causal claims are they? Who makes the claims you have listed—the author or the sources she cites?

Answers will vary.

Is the origin of the causal claims important in how you or other readers might evaluate the strength or validity of the selection's arguments? Why or why not?

The origins of the claims are important because the reader will be evaluating them in an effort to gauge the credibility of the author.

How do these causal claims advance its argument(s)? (For a discussion of causal arguments, see Chapter 10.)

Answers will vary.

4. This selection contains two very different visual arguments — a photo collage and a complex set of "country profiles" that provide several kinds of information about Nigeria, India, Indonesia, and Brazil—both reproduced from the original version of the piece. What does each contribute to the selection? (In other words, do you think you would have read or understood the selection differently had one or both of these visual arguments not been included? How so?) Study the information given in the country profiles. Make a list of the kinds of information each country profile gives. Why is this information useful and appropriate, given the focus of the selection?

Each country profile adds to the reader's understanding of religious growth around the world. The profiles include the number of members and the percentage of growth of groups such as Christians (Protestants, Anglicans, Catholics), Muslims, Animists, Hindus, Independents, New Religionists, and Spiritists, according to the religions that are represented in each country. This information is useful in visualizing the growth of religion around the world.

What functions do the circles of different sizes play in communicating information? How do the illustrations contribute to this visual argument?

The circles of different sizes show the relative size of the religious community without using percentages. The illustrations give a concise view of religion around the world and create a context for the article.

5. Create a country profile like the ones given here for the United States and one other country of your choosing (other than the four given here). Be sure to include the sources of your information. When you have completed this assignment, compare your profile for the United States with those created by two classmates. If there are differences, seek to locate the cause(s) of those differences: for example, did you rely on different sources for the basic information you used, or did you classify, combine, or represent the information you found in different ways?

Answers will vary.

6. Writing assignment

Classroom Exercise: focus on the argument

Are students surprised to hear that the modern world is becoming more religious? What current world events might be influencing such independent movements? How many students in the class are involved in a religious organization? Do students think that college students are more or less likely than other populations to be active in this way? Is age a factor? Is academic education a factor? What do students think about evangelization on campus? What do they think might be the best way to reach students with a spiritual or religious message?

Pew Global Attitudes Project *Among Wealthy Nations . . . , U.S. Stands Alone in Its Embrace of Religion* pp. 851–853

1. Does the information contained in this brief introductory section to the Pew Global Attitudes Project surprise you in any way? Why or why not? In your opinion, what might account for the unusual attitudes and behavior of Americans in comparison to citizens of other wealthy nations that the United States often sees as its peers and allies?

Answers will vary.

2. What do we learn about China, Egypt, Jordan, and Lebanon in this text? Why might these governments not want their citizens discussing religion? (You may need to do some research to find out something about these countries, their demographic makeup, and their history.)

Briefly, Egypt, Jordan, and Lebanon are all nations in which religious beliefs and differences have sparked wars and continued bloodshed. China's official religious stance is atheist because the government believes that religion encourages disloyalty and subversion.

3. As mentioned in the headnote, social scientists often rely on charts, tables, figures, and diagrams to do much of their work for them. Not only do they generally contain a great deal of information that is never discussed explicitly in the text, but they also permit the reader to check conclusions drawn in the text against the visual display, whether it is a chart (like the ones used in this excerpt) or a table, figure, or diagram. What sorts of additional observations not already mentioned in the text can you make on the basis of information included in the two charts?

(The second chart, "Poor Nations Very Religious, Wealthy Are Less So . . . Except for the U.S.," may be difficult for you to read at first. It represents the results of the correlation, or statistical relationship, between wealth, as measured by annual per capita income, and the importance reportedly placed on religion, as measured in terms of percentage of answers of "very important" to the question given in footnote 1. The horizontal sloping line in the chart, the regression line, represents a perfect negative correlation: if greater wealth in a country always meant comparably less importance reportedly attached to religion, all the dots or data points, each representing a country, would fall along this line. The closer the data point representing a country is to the line, the tighter the negative relationship between the wealth and importance of religion. Outliers, those data points farthest from the regression line, represent exceptions — for example, Vietnam and the United States in this case.)

Answers will vary. One question sparked by the first chart is, What factors account for the significant differences in responses among the countries of Western Europe — Great Britain, Italy, Germany, and France? One observation of the

second chart is that there were consistent low-percentage responses along the entire income range, whereas the high-percentage responses were grouped mainly in the lowest income bracket.

4. Writing assignment

Classroom Exercise: focus on research

Choose two countries from the study that had significantly different responses but are located in a similar region (some pairs might include Vietnam and Indonesia, Argentina and Guatemala, Uzbekistan and Pakistan, the Czech Republic and Poland, and Canada and the United States). Research each country's religious history, and create an argument for why the two countries offered such disparate responses to the survey. What are their most significant similarities and differences? What factors besides income influence their religious leanings? See Chapter 19 for guidelines for effective research strategies.

Michelle Bryant   *Selling Safe Sex in Public*
Schools   pp. 854–858

1. What sort of ethos does Shelby Knox create for herself during the interview reported here? What role(s) does her faith play in that ethos?

   Shelby Knox creates an ethos of credibility because she is a young Christian woman who is not sexually active and who contends that sex education is the only way to provide important information to other young people.

   Would her narrative or ethos be different if Knox were an atheist? Why or why not? (For a discussion of ethos, see Chapter 3.)

   If Knox were an atheist, we might not be as surprised by her stance, and her argument would not resonate as strongly with the audience.

2. What causal arguments do we find in the narrative of Shelby Knox's experiences?

   Knox contends that by not teaching youth about safe sex, society is contributing to unwanted pregnancies and sexually transmitted diseases. She also argues that the youth

commission's sex education campaign was a major factor in reducing STDs and teen pregnancy.

Why are these arguments crucial to the argument made by the selection? (For a discussion of causal arguments, see Chapter 10.)

These causal arguments support Knox's larger argument that sex education is necessary for teens.

3. In paragraph 15, Knox contends, "I think God wants you to question." What does Knox want people of faith to question? Why?

Knox wants people to question religious tenets that call for people to turn their backs on people in need—such as sexually active teens who are confused and gay students who feel the effects of discrimination. She argues that "God loves everyone" and that as a Christian she should work to serve those in need.

Why do you imagine Knox believes "he [God] can't use blind followers"? (Obviously, Knox is using "blind" metaphorically in this case.)

Followers who do not think for themselves risk contradicting their own beliefs and missing opportunities to be of use to humanity.

4. This article appeared in *Life & Letters: A Publication of the College of Liberal Arts of the University of Texas at Austin*, a magazine that highlights the research and achievements of faculty and students in the college. It is distributed within the college and to its friends and supporters, including donors, many of whom would be politically conservative and would identify as evangelical Christians. How can we see awareness of the magazine's intended audience in the selection of Shelby Knox as the topic of an article? In the way her story is presented?

The article takes a respectful tone and does not directly criticize the local government or Christians for their beliefs. Knox's story is told factually, and any criticisms are quotes from Knox herself.

How might the selection challenge readers holding various political or religious beliefs? How do the illustrations contribute to the article's argument?

Knox's position may be in opposition to many of the readers of the magazines, and her argumentation might challenge some of their deeply held beliefs. The pictures in the article show a young woman who appears professional and clean-cut. Her family is pictured with both parents. Her father is wearing an American flag shirt, which reiterates her family's traditional values.

5. Writing assignment

Classroom Exercise: focus on the argument

Both sides of the sexual education controversy claim to have scientific evidence that a particular program (abstinence only or safe sex) significantly influences the occurrence of sexually transmitted diseases and unwanted pregnancies. Why might this topic be controversial? What suggestions do students have for helping to avoid emotional responses to the issue? How do race, class, and religion affect the discussion? If parents are unwilling or unable to discuss safe sex with their children, who, if anyone, should be available to guide students with questions?

Naomi Schaefer Riley Introduction to *God on the Quad: How Religious Colleges and the Missionary Generation Are Changing America* pp. 859–871

1. In this selection, Riley tells readers a great deal about the methodology she used in conducting her study with respect to selecting both categories of schools and kinds of schools. She also gives readers a list of the specific questions she sought to answer. How is this information helpful and even necessary to the reader of her research?

   Riley's questions lay out the basis for her investigation. Each question plays into how these students are different from young people at nonreligious schools and what they have to offer the world when they finish.

2. What does Riley tell us about her identity, including her own religious and political beliefs? (In interviews about her work, she has identified herself as a Conservative Jew.) Is this information useful or necessary for the reader? Why might she have included this

information near the end of the "Introduction" rather than else-where in the piece? Are there strategic advantages to her choice? Potential disadvantages?

The author shares that she grew up in states that are pre-dominantly Democratic and attended secular schools. This information is interesting because it creates an ethos of dis-interested reporting. Presenting this information at the end of the section is useful because it allows the reader to un-derstand the point of the book and argumentation before learning about the author herself. A potential disadvantage is that the reader may have been questioning the author's credibility before arriving at the end and learning about the author.

3. In what historical, social, and political contexts does Riley place her research? How is her research an outgrowth of or a response to these contexts?

Riley shares that she began her research on September 10, 2001. Because the September 11 attacks in New York, Penn-sylvania, and Washington, D.C. were carried out by men who claimed to be devout Muslims, religion became an im-portant part of the discussion about national security in the weeks following that day. Her research was probably al-tered or enhanced because of these conditions.

4. Riley makes much of the contrast between the terms *spiritual* and *religious*. What definitions does she and those she studied provide for each?

Riley clearly distinguishes between spirituality, a "feel-good" substitute, and religion, a systematic practice based on devotion to a creator who acts on a person's behalf.

Might her argument have been different if she had acknowledged that many who prefer the term *spiritual* to *religious* do so because of the negative connotations of the latter, which are linked to its as-sociation with fundamentalists of an especially narrow-minded sort?

Her argument would have been different if she acknowl-edged the negative connotations connected to the term *religious*. Then she would have had to admit that some stu-

164

dents were religious in the sense that she uses it but that they do not express their actions by using that particular word.

5. Writing assignment

Classroom Exercise: focus on the argument

Riley did not visit public universities or private universities that are unaffiliated with a specific faith. This was not the focus of her research. Do students think that a "missionary generation" is active only at the religious institutions that Riley profiles? Could a larger movement toward spirituality and volunteerism be growing among university students? Members of the baby-boom generation often complain that today's young men and women are not as invested as they were in politics and social justice. What does the class think about this accusation? Are students more selfish, more focused, or just living in different times? Have students write a statement about the state of college students' social responsibility and spiritual life and then reflect on how they see themselves in comparison to the majority. (It may be interesting to see how students see the average college student in comparison to themselves.)

Elisabeth Bumiller *Preaching to the Choir?*
 Not This Time pp. 872–875

1. What are Elisabeth Bumiller's goals in writing this text? How would you characterize her arguments in terms of stasis theory? (For a discussion of stasis theory, see Chapter 1.)

   Bumiller presents a news story about the happenings at Calvin College surrounding its invitation to President George W. Bush to speak. Her argument is one of definition as she characterizes the nature of the conflict and debate.

2. Bumiller's subject is the controversy surrounding a college commencement address. First, why are such addresses called "commencement addresses"? Should we expect such speeches to represent forensic, epideictic, or deliberative occasions for argument? (For a discussion of these categories of occasions for argument, see Chapter 1.)

   Commencement addresses take place at commencement or graduation exercises. On this day, graduates will commence

or begin their new careers with their degrees. These addresses are often deliberative because the speaker is addressing the graduates about their future.

Why? Based on this article, how do politicians and political strategists see such events? University administrators? Graduate students and their families? Why?

Politicians and strategists see these addresses as opportunities to align themselves with certain voters or constituents. University administrators invite important or interesting people to address their graduates as a way to bring attention to the school. Families and graduates look forward to having a notable speaker as well to mark their day of achievement.

3. Bumiller contends that Christians, even evangelical Christians, aren't monolithic. How and why is such a claim contrary to popular discourse about religion and politics in American life?

Christians, especially evangelical Christians, are often stereotyped as conservative and even out of touch with modern society. Calvin College poses a challenge to this idea.

4. Bumiller reports that many students wore buttons proclaiming, "God is not a Democrat or a Republican." What argument do such buttons make? How is their meaning linked to the immediate context at Calvin College? To the larger context of American political and public life in 2005?

Theses buttons argue that Christian students are not necessarily Republicans. The students wanted to remind those watching that they do not necessarily agree with the politics of President Bush, even though he was giving the commencement address at their college. The current political climate has often linked Republican politics, the war in Iraq, and American patriotism with Christianity.

5. Writing assignment

Classroom Exercise: focus on the argument

What makes Bumiller's article newsworthy? Why would the public be interested in the reaction to a speech given by President George W.

Bush on a college campus? Why is it important to publicize situations such as this one? Why is the choice of a commencement speaker an important one? What is the best-case scenario for a commencement address from the point of view of all involved? In a later selection, we hear the college president's reaction to Bush's address, but how do students think that Bush himself viewed the entire situation? Can students find any public record from the Office of the President about his visit to Calvin College?

Concerned Faculty, Staff, and Emeriti of Calvin College   *An Open Letter to the President of the United States of America, George W. Bush*   pp. 876–877

1. What argument(s) does this letter make?

   The letter's authors argue that George W. Bush does not embody the Christianity that they profess.

2. You can analyze this letter as an example of Rogerian argumentation, which seeks to acknowledge and build on common ground (in contrast, say, to highlighting or exacerbating differences between parties). Where in the text do we find efforts to acknowledge and build on shared assumptions, beliefs, or premises?

   The opening and closing paragraphs seek to make an alliance with Bush as a Christian.

3. At the same time, it is clear that those who signed this letter disagreed profoundly with President Bush and invoke their religious beliefs as justifications — or even warrants — for those disagreements. We can therefore characterize the letter as an argument of definition, one that contrasts competing understandings of Christian belief. What specific definitional criteria are enumerated in the letter? (For a discussion of arguments of definitions, see Chapter 8.)

   This letter presents a discussion of the nature of Christianity by enumerating four points of contention with the President's actions. The argument includes a claim of definition, a general definition of key concepts, and examples as evidence for each point.

4. How might Christians who support President Bush respond to this letter? You may wish to offer responses (or even rebuttals) to the criteria listed or offer additional criteria not mentioned here. If you

feel that you are not familiar enough with the tenets of Christianity or with liberal and conservative approaches to Christianity, work with classmates who are in answering this question or use the Internet to research this topic.

Answers will vary.

5. Writing assignment

Classroom Exercise: focus on rhetoric

How does the visual shape of the argument contribute to its effectiveness? When creating a succinct argument, what do students see as the most important consideration? This letter is addressed to President Bush, but it is an open letter. Who might be the intended audience of such a letter? How might the argumentation in the letter change if it was revised to be read by the public?

Gaylen J. Byker   *Reflections on the 2005 Commencement*   pp. 878–883

1. How does Gaylen J. Byker construct and evaluate President Bush's visit to his campus? What arguments is he making? In what ways do they reflect and result from his role as president of the college?

   The president of the college describes the U.S. President's visit as overwhelmingly positive. He argues that it was a great honor for the university and that students handled any differences well. Most readers would expect a positive review of this event by a college administrator. The administration has much invested in the school reputation.

2. What sort of evidence does Byker use as he develops his argument? How does he rely on personal testimony in particular? Why is personal testimony especially effective in contexts like this one? (For a discussion of kinds of evidence, see Chapter 16.)

   Ryder relies on his own observations, reported comments, and a letter from a parent that he includes in his article. Personal statements from those involved in the occasion stand as strong evidence in favor of their report. An eyewitness is always more credible that a secondhand report.

3. How does Byker define and characterize "convicted civility"? How does he use this concept to build his argument? How does "con-

victed civility" relate to Rogerian argumentation, discussed in Chapter 1 and question 2 on p. 874.

"Convicted civility" is a gracious and intense passion for one's beliefs. Ryder uses this definition to illustrate how the students reacted to the President's address. Convicted civility means remaining calm enough in your beliefs in one side of an argument to hear the other side and see the common ground that exists.

4. Writing assignment

Classroom Exercise: focus on the world

President Byker's public reflections are reminiscent of many official documents that are published by universities and other institutions. How often have students read a university publication that frankly discusses a deficiency of that institution or takes responsibility for a negative situation on campus? Why might universities and other institutions hesitate to admit to or recognize any negative situations involving their facilities, students, or employees? What makes universities, even private ones, political institutions?

John Zwier *An Opportunity for Intelligent Debate* pp. 884–886

1. In what ways is John Zwier's argument a proposal argument? What is his specific proposal? What steps led him to make that proposal? In other words, in what ways has he considered questions of definition, cause, and evaluation before offering his proposal? (For a discussion of proposal arguments, see Chapter 11.)

   Zwier proposes that students remain respectful during the commencement address and express their protest by wearing buttons provided by the school. Zwier shares that he considered not protesting until he decided that aligning the school with Bush might not be wise. This involved considering definitions of religion and politics, the possible meanings of the President's visit, and the current conflict at the college.

2. Zwier comments that the button's statement—a visual argument—isn't divisive (paragraph 9). Do you agree or disagree? Why? How

would wearing such a button compare with boycotting graduation as a form of argument? Why?

Answers will vary.

3. Clearly, one of Zwier's concerns is the association of "Christianity with the Republican Party . . . whether it's justified or not" (paragraph 4). Zwier later explains that wearing the button provides students and faculty "the opportunity to express their hope that President George W. Bush does not politicize religion during the Commencement ceremony of 2005" (paragraph 6). What does it mean to "politicize religion"?

"Politicizing religion" means aligning a religion and a political movement in a one-to-one relationship or suggesting that members of one organization should or should not participate in the actions of another.

Did those who signed "An Open Letter to the President . . ." likely believe they were politicizing religion? Why or why not?

Those who wrote the letter probably thought that they were resisting the politicization of religion by addressing Bush before his visit.

Is it possible or beneficial *not* to politicize religion in American society or any society? Why or why not?

Answers will vary.

4. Writing assignment

Classroom Exercise: focus on the argument

Is Zwier's writing style typical of what students have read in their own student newspaper? What tone does Zwier use? Have students write a letter about the graduation to the editor of the Calvin College paper. They should write it as if they were a Calvin student. Students should pay attention to the tone of thei letter, the ethos that they want to create for themselves, the succinctness and readability of their text, and the type of argument that they are creating.

Antonin Scalia *God's Justice and Ours* pp. 887–893

1. Justice Scalia devotes the first part of this article to distinguishing between those who read the Constitution as a "living document,"

the meaning of which changes as society "matures," and those who see it as "enduring," with a focus on its meaning at the time it was drafted. What, for Scalia, are the characteristics and consequences of each view?

Those who view the Constitution as a living document believe that Supreme Court decisions must take into account our current conceptions of morality and decency and that therefore our interpretations of the Constitution evolve throughout time. Those who view the Constitution as enduring believe that justices must judge cases based on the definitions implied when the Constitution was written; their boundaries of morality and legality exist today unless modified by the legislative branch of the government.

Which of the two views do you prefer? Why? Does either one leave you uncomfortable? Why or why not?

Answers will vary.

2. Throughout the article, Scalia makes other important distinctions: cases in which the state (that is, the government) decrees death versus those where it does not restrain death from occurring (paragraph 5), private morality versus governmental morality (paragraph 10), European versus American attitudes toward religion in public life (paragraph 14), legal versus moral matters (paragraph 17), and Christian versus post-Freudian secularist perspectives on death (paragraph 15), among others. Choose two such distinctions, and specify the basis of the distinction (in each case, a kind of definition—see Chapter 8).

Answers will vary. For one example, Scalia notes that while for post-Freudian secularists death is the end of existence and thus a cataclysmic punishment, for Christians death leads to the next phase of existence and thus is not the literal end of the world.

3. Scalia concludes by claiming that it is a good thing for American Catholics (and, by extension, people of any faith in the United States) to be involved in aspects of public and political life. Do you agree or disagree? Why?

Answers will vary.

4. Scalia argues that a justice who finds the death penalty immoral should resign from the bench (paragraph 8). Do you agree or disagree? Why? Whatever your stance, you'll need to do your best to anticipate and acknowledge potential rebuttals against your position.

Answers will vary.

5. Writing assignment

Classroom Exercise: focus on the argument

Justice Scalia's comparison of religion in the United States with that in Europe corroborates the conclusions reached in the second reading of this chapter, the Pew Global Attitudes Project's report, "Among Wealthy Nations . . ." (pp. 851–853). Each uses significantly different sources of evidence to draw and present conclusions. Using Chapter 16, "What Counts as Evidence," as a guide, analyze the types of evidence each uses and how they contribute to the author's argument. Consider as well which lines of argument (arguments from the heart, from values, from character, from facts and reason) each reading employs and why.

Randy Cohen   *Between the Sexes*   pp. 894–896

1. Do you agree or disagree with Randy Cohen's analysis of the situation J.L. describes? In other words, did the Orthodox Jew's refusal to shake hands with a woman who wasn't a relative by blood or marriage constitute an act of sexism in terms of the intentions of the real estate agent or its effect upon his client? Should J.L., as Cohen suggests, have torn up the contract? Why or why not?

Answers will vary.

2. Evaluate the response to Cohen's column. What sorts of arguments—those from the heart, those based on character, or those based on fact and reason—do these letter writers use?

Answers will vary but may include the following examples. Cara Weinstein Rosenthal uses an argument based on character when she defines herself as "a Jew, a feminist and a future rabbi." In addition, she makes an argument based on facts and reason when she defines the strictures of "shomer negiah" to show how they don't fit Cohen's assessment. Robert M. Gottesman uses an argument based on values when he notes that "Religious freedom is a constitutional

and moral right." **Helen Pogrin uses an argument from the heart when she argues that the real estate agent's refusal to shake hands was "out of respect to his own wife and to other women."**

Which specific arguments do you find most persuasive? Why?

Answers will vary.

3. Writing assignment

Classroom Exercise: focus on the argument

Who is Randy Cohen, and why do we trust his ethical advice? Conduct research as a class to find out about his background, his credentials, and his writing and publishing history. How did he come to be "The Ethicist"? How does his title, rather than his name, function as an argument based on character? How does your knowledge of him as a person affect your trust in his advice? Read some of his other columns, and discuss his advice. Do you frequently agree with him? Do you disagree? What are the main issues on which your opinion differs from Cohen's?

Mariam Rahmani *Wearing a Head Scarf Is My Choice as a Muslim; Please Respect It* pp. 897–900

1. What is Mariam Rahmani's argument? How does she define the meaning of wearing the *hijab* and justify it?

   Rahmani's argument is that women should have the right to wear a hijab if they choose to. She defines wearing a hijab as a self-reminder to focus on developing her inner self rather than her outer self.

   How effectively does she anticipate and respond to potential counterarguments?

   Answers will vary.

2. How does Rahmani call into question Western notions of "liberation" for women?

   She dismisses Western notions of liberation for women as having resulted in objectification and pressure to be beautiful. Rahmani argues that Western-style liberation is not necessarily a positive for women.

3. If women of any faith or no faith at all believe that they're regarded by men or society at large for their "physicality," should they have to take action, or should men or society change? Why? How?

Answers will vary.

4. Rahmani sets up a strong contrast between the West and Islam, yet she is, based on available evidence, a Muslim in and of the West. If we assume this statement is true, has Rahmani contradicted herself or weakened her argument? In other words, must there be a strong contrast between Islam and the West? Why or why not?

Answers will vary.

5. In paragraph 13, Rahmani contends that we must "agree to disagree." Do you agree with her position, or are there alternatives she has not mentioned? What might they be?

Answers will vary.

6. Writing assignment

Classroom Exercise: focus on the argument

A common argument against hijabs and other veils is the value of assimilation within a secular society. Many non-Muslims argue that the veil creates a barrier between Western cultures and the women and families of Islam. How might the veil create a social distance? Who should have to bear the burden of change in a situation such as this? Is assimilation the best answer? How does this question of hijabs compare to the wearing of yarmulkes, crosses, sacred medals, and other religious icons? At what point, if any, does a religious garment or adornment separate a person from other people?

Ad Council *A Priest, a Rabbi, and an Imam Are Walking Down the Street*   pp. 901–902

1. How would you summarize the argument(s) made by this advertisement? Imagine trying to explain the argument(s) to someone from another country — France, for example. (See the previous selection, Mariam Rahmani's "Wearing a Head Scarf Is My Choice . . . ," for more information on how France deals with religious differences among its citizens.)

This ad argues that we can learn to live together without giving up our religious differences.

How would you describe what's distinctly American about the argument(s) being made here?

This argument is American in the sense that America purports to tolerate and even enjoy differences among its people. Rather than pushing assimilation, the ad presents acceptance of difference as the path to peace.

2. The advertisement begins, "A priest, a rabbi, and an imam are walking down the street. (There's no punchline.)" What sorts of cultural knowledge do the ad's creators expect the reader to bring to the text? How does the sentence "There's no punchline" disrupt expectations readers might have? Which genre is associated with such an opening? How does the ad's beginning in this way contribute to its message?

This is the usual set-up for a joke based on religious stereotypes, and readers would expect a punch line after the set-up. The fact that there is no punch line contradicts the reader's expectations. Readers need to be familiar with this type of joke to see the strength of the message. The disjuncture between the first sentence and the second one causes the reader to pause and consider the message.

3. This advertisement claims, "Because we [Americans] are free to choose which religion, if any, we'd like to follow, it enables us to have a deeper, more personal relationship with our faith than would otherwise be possible." Do you agree or disagree? Why? How would America likely be different if it did have a state religion or if, as in some countries, only a single religion could be practiced?

Answers will vary.

4. In what ways is this advertisement a proposal argument? In what ways are all advertisements proposal arguments? (For a discussion of proposal arguments, see Chapter 11.)

The ad proposes that we all try to be more tolerant of each others' views. All advertising is aimed at proposing some action on the part of the viewer.

5. Writing assignment

Classroom Exercise: focus on the argument

Do students think that the average American is as respectful and accepting of other religions as this advertisement might reflect? Even in a free society where we may choose the religion (if any) that we want to practice, what might keep persons from different religions from understanding each other or becoming friends? What issues do Americans need to confront about issues of religion and perhaps other issues in U.S. social life that affect tolerance? Have students create a cartoon that represents their understanding of religion in America, whatever that might be. Have students share with the class to compare perceptions.

Making a Visual Argument: Public Service Campaigns for Religious Tolerance

U.S. Department of Justice   *Common Muslim American Head Coverings*

The SikhNetwork   *Sikhs: Proud to Be Americans*

Anti-Defamation League   *Anti-Semitism Is Anti-Me*   pp. 903–908

1. The previous selection, "A Priest, a Rabbi, and an Imam Are Walking Down the Street . . ." congratulated Americans on creating a country where people of various religious beliefs can live and work in harmony. If that argument is valid, why do the arguments given here exist at all?

   Answers will vary.

2. Why might the U.S. government create visual arguments like "Common Muslim American Head Coverings"? What's their purpose? Their value?

   The government may hope to educate people about Americans who are different from themselves in an effort to increase tolerance. It might be news to some people that the head coverings included in the poster are Muslim.

   What specific roles do the visual elements of the poster play? Would verbal descriptions have been as effective as images are?

The visuals provide examples for the message, but they also humanize a minority group that the majority may have little contact with. Verbal description would not have had as much of an impact, and it would not have been visually inviting.

How does the information at the bottom of the poster—"Some images and descriptions of Muslim head coverings provided by the American Arab Anti-Discrimination Committee (ADC)" — contribute its credibility? Its ethos?

The citation contributes to the credibility of the poster and to the ethos of an informed ad.

3. Describe the images included in "Sikhs: Proud to Be Americans." Why might these images have been chosen? In other words, what sorts of Sikhs are represented here, and what sorts of appeals does their presence represent? How does the repeated image of the Statue of Liberty across the bottom of the poster contribute to its message?

The Sikh poster shows men and women in their traditional headdresses, which were probably chosen to represent variations within the religion. The Statue of Liberty adds to the argument that these people are Americans.

What are the functions of this visual argument? Who is the audience? Why?

This argument is probably meant for non-Sikh Americans who do not know how to identify Sikhs and often confuse them with Arabs.

4. What role do the two images included in the "Anti-Semitism Is Anti-Me" advertisements play? Why might these images have been chosen? What sorts of appeals do they represent? Why?

The two images are of Jewish people who do not look like typical Jews. They may have been used to show variations within the Jewish community and remind audiences that they cannot always guess a person's background.

What sorts of images might you have expected in such ads? How does the contrast between viewer expectation and the ads themselves contribute to their effectiveness? In what sense is anti-Semitism (or any form of discrimination) "anti-everybody"?

The viewer would expect a photo of someone of Eastern European descent and maybe even a Hassidic Jew as the "quintessential Jewish person." Discrimination is often based on stereotypes and features that cannot be tied to only one group or to everyone in a group. Discrimination doesn't let the viewer see a person.

Is such a claim true universally, or is there some aspect of this issue that is particularly relevant to the American context? Why?

Answers will vary.

5. Writing assignment

Classroom Exercise: focus on the argument

What other groups in the United States are misunderstood or misrepresented? Have students choose a different minority group—whether ethnic, social, or other—and have them design a poster or flyer that confronts common stereotypes or presents an uncommon image to viewers.

Azar Nafisi   *Mysterious Connections That Link Us Together*   pp. 909–911

1. What arguments is Azar Nafisi making in this commentary? How would you characterize them—as arguments based on reason and facts? Emotions? Character and values? (For a discussion of kinds of arguments, see Chapters 2–4.)

   Nafisi argues that empathy allows people to challenge rigid beliefs and feel the suffering of others. This is an argument of values and emotion. Nafisi shares the story of Huck Finn and a story of her own about a time when she was the recipient of such empathy. Nafisi shares a glimpse into her own character by recognizing that her students acted courageously when they defended her.

2. In this commentary, Nafisi combines a literary example, personal experience, and current events to make her argument(s). How does she weave these together? What are the relationships among them?

   Nafisi uses empathy as her central theme and strings together each part of her argument by reiterating Huck Finn's mention of hell.

3. What is the significance of Nafisi's title? What sorts of "mysterious connections" linking people together do you see evidence of in her essay?

"Mysterious connections" are the unlikely commonalities that link us to people with whom we would not imagine that we have anything in common. Nafisi gives the example of a young white boy (Finn) and a runaway black slave (Jim) that he helps. She also mentions an experience that she had as a liberal professor of conservative students in Iran.

4. Imagine a conversation between Nafisi, Mariam Rahmani (author of "Wearing a Head Scarf Is My Choice . . ."), and Shelby Knox, who is featured in Michelle Bryant's "Selling Safe Sex in Public Schools" earlier in this chapter. How might religion and religious beliefs figure into that conversation?

If Nafisi, Rahmani, and Knox had a discussion, religion would be mentioned because each speaks about tolerance for those that are different, especially those who hold a different religious stance.

What might these women agree on?

Knox would readily agree that Huck Finn did the right thing in condemning himself to "Hell." Nafisi would probably agree that "God loves everyone" and that we should work to help the least among us. Rahmani talks more about tolerance that proactively reaches out to others, but she would agree that accepting others' differences is key to living together.

Would there be things they might agree to disagree about?

Rahmani and Nafisi would probably disagree about what it means to wear the hijab, but perhaps they would agree to accept each other's decisions.

5. Writing assignment

Classroom Exercise: focus on the argument

Nafisi mentions two students who spoke on her behalf when she was expelled from her university in Tehran. These two students were far more conservative than Nafisi and had debated with her at length in her classes. Students often have negative feelings about a professor with whom they have debated. Why might the conservative students have chosen to defend a liberal teacher when she was expelled for breaking religious laws that the students probably supported? Later readings will address minority views in academia, but here reflect on how students generally react to a professor with strong political beliefs and how those professors present their views when they are pertinent to the subject at hand.

Wrap-Up Exercises for Constructing Arguments about Religion and Public Life

These three activities are suggested as wrap-up exercises in which students integrate any or all of the readings of the chapter. In addition, exercises 1 and 2 would be suitable for an in-class essay assignment.

1. Construct an argument for the use of violence as an appropriate response to particular issues. The violence could be symbolic (for example, shouting a speaker down, not permitting certain subjects to be discussed publicly) or real (for example, responding with physical violence). In your essay, you will need to delimit clearly the circumstances under which you contend a violent response is justified and the nature of the violent response that you believe to be justifiable. You will also need to assess the consequences for all involved — the one(s) silenced or attacked, the silencer(s) or attacker(s), and society at large (especially because our society permits freedom of expression but acknowledges that its members hold a range of opinions on most issues).

2. Write an essay in which you delimit the boundaries of either freedom of expression or freedom of religion in this society. Be sure to provide justifications for any boundaries you set and discuss the consequences of accepting them for individuals and for society at large. If you contend that there should be no boundaries on freedom of expression or religion, justify your position by describing how to resolve conflicts that might arise with respect to the expression of ideas (or manner of their expression) or of religious beliefs. (One way to approach these subjects may be to ask yourself whether there are certain topics or ways of arguing that should not be permitted in this society or whether there are certain ritual practices that should not be permitted in the name of religion. Infant

sacrifice, for example, would likely be an example of the latter for all Americans, though the practice occurred in times past in certain societies.)

3. Rewrite one of the arguments you've written for this course that required you to take an explicit stance on a particular issue. If the original argument was primarily agonistic, the rewritten essay should be invitational. If the original argument was primarily invitational, the new version should be agonistic. As you'll discover, this assignment is more complex than it might appear at first glance. Such revisions typically require not only a shift in tone but also changes with respect to the kinds of support used and even the statement of the thesis itself.

CHAPTER 27

What Should "Diversity on Campus" Mean?

At one time *diversity* meant allowing women to study with men at the college level. Women now outnumber men in many universities, even though certain majors continue to be dominated by males. After decades of discrimination against students of color, schools still struggle to attract minority scholars. Currently, the same rhetoric that was used to argue for support for female and minority scholars is now being used to argue for stronger conservative representation on campus. Some claim that this is a worthy effort to pursue to expose students to different points of view. But are all opinions equal? We strive to include students of diverse backgrounds to enrich the learning environment and to assure that one group of people is not dominating the educated class expressly because we believe that people are equal. But what if certain ideologies take hold of academia? And how real is purposeful, calculated diversity? The readings in this cluster invite us to consider what problems need to be fixed and what actions should be taken to fix them. This consideration leads us to ask the following questions:

- Why might these situations exist, and what (if anything) should universities do to change these facts?
- If diversity in general is seen as a laudable goal, how far should we broaden our understanding of *diversity*? Should every public institution be representative of the U.S. population in race? Gender? Political ideology? Religion? What characteristics are the most important to balance? Why?
- Schools still talk about diversity and affirmative action, but there is a large movement to remove any preferential admission or hiring programs for minorities of any type. What are the disadvantages of these programs? What alternatives are there to affirmative action programs?

Making a Visual Argument: Student-Made Diversity Posters

James Sanders *A Universe Within*

Stephanie Heyman *Everyone A Part, No One Apart*

Heidi Small *Lives Woven Together*

Alyson Jones *What's Your View?*

Megan Stampfli *Embrace Diversity*

Carolyn Woito *Breaking Boxes, Building Bridges* pp. 916–922

1. Which of these visual arguments do you find most appealing? Least appealing? Why?

   Answers will vary.

2. Analyze the relationship between text—the words used—and the visual images and layout in each of the posters. What's the interaction between the text, on the one hand, and the visual images and layout, on the other, in each one?

   "A Universe Within" uses text to title this piece. "Everyone A Part . . ." uses words to create a message in collage form. "Lives Woven Together" uses text as a title and in prose to complement the painting. "What's Your View?" has a title and uses two different color fonts to create a message in the picture and several smaller messages around the main poster. "Embrace Diversity" uses words in collage form mixed over a picture to finish the sentence "Diversity Is . . . ." Finally, "Breaking Boxes . . ." has words labeling different aspects of the picture and a variety of nouns at the bottom that are associated with diversity.

   Which poster is most effective in this regard? Why?

   Answers will vary.

3. If you take each of these posters to be a definitional argument, defining diversity in some way, what arguments is each making? In other words, how does each poster define diversity? (For a discussion of definitional arguments, see Chapter 8.)

The posters, respectively, define diversity as the many parts of one whole, inclusion, tapestry, the absence of bias, the acceptance of others, and seeing beyond stereotypes.

4. In defining and commenting on the notion of diversity, these posters range from approaching their topic in a didactic fashion (that is, seeking to teach a moral lesson) to approaching it much more vaguely. (Note the evaluative — and potentially negative — connotations the labels "didactic" and "vague" carry.) Choose the posters that you find most explicitly didactic and those that you find most vague in their approach to the topic. Justify your choices. Which approach do you prefer? Why? Which do you believe is more effective in situations like this one? Why?

   Answers will vary.

5. Writing assignment

6. Writing assignment

Classroom Exercise: focus on rhetoric

Having evaluated the different posters by answering the questions at the end of the chapter, students should be aware of what they thought was effective and what wasn't. Have students create a "call for posters" that announces a poster contest at their own school. They should include a list of requirements or tips for a quality poster that will draw student attention. Students should share their requirements and discuss their own experiences with school-sponsored public service ads (they might be memorable ones, inappropriate ones, or even "lame" ones.)

Sarah Karnasiewicz   *The Campus Crusade for Guys*   pp. 923–930

1. What argument(s) is Karnasiewicz making with respect to the nature of diversity on campus?

   Karnasiewicz is arguing that many colleges are seeing an increase in the proportion of females to males.

   How persuasive do you find them? Why? Should there be affirmative action for men? Why or why not?

   Answers will vary.

2. Although this article is about gender, it's also about issues of race or ethnicity and class as well as the intersection of these social variables. What sorts of observations or claims are made about each of these variables in the article?

The crusade for boys is similar to affirmative action for minorities at the university level. Like affirmative action, some pundits argue that preparing boys for college needs to start in elementary education. The author also points out that the disproportionate achievement of boys is even stronger in lower socioeconomic levels. If schools are failing young men, then we certainly need to look at the poorest school districts.

Do you agree or disagree? Do you find any of the claims made about these topics troubling? Why or why not?

Answers will vary.

3. How and why are females and males stigmatized by a lack of education or by the kind of job they might hold?

Uneducated women tend to hold lower-paying jobs than uneducated men do. Those men are more likely to be in skilled-labor positions while women are in service industries. As the author notes, women can be stigmatized for having too much education, and while pundits discuss a possible "dearth" of educated men for these educated women to marry, no one was concerned that men would not have educated partners back when they were the larger school population.

Although it isn't mentioned, in what ways might the marriage market encourage young women to attend college (or even to succeed academically, more broadly)?

College is a good place to meet an educated husband. On the other hand, if women want to prepare themselves to be self-sufficient in case marriage does not work out for them, college also provides good training.

4. What's the allusion in Karnasiewicz's title? (If you need a hint, check out <http://ccci.org>.) How and why is it appropriate, given the subject matter of the article?

The Campus Crusade for Christ is a national Christian organization for university students. The club name is generally well known on campuses, and the title of this article takes advantage of that notoriety.

Is the allusion risky in any way? Why or why not?

This play on words is witty, but it may offend some students.

5. Among the kinds of evidence that Karnasiewicz uses effectively is statistics. Where and how does she and those she cites use statistics advantageously?

The author and those she cites use statistics to show how many schools have far more men than women. We don't see numbers for schools that have equal numbers of men and women.

In what ways does she qualify claims made on the basis of statistical data? How does qualifying arguments in this way contribute to Karnasiewicz's ethos? (For a discussion of using facts ilke statistics, see Chapter 4; for a discussion of ethos, see Chapter 3.)

Karnasiewicz questions whether the statistics about college men tell the whole story. Men still earn more than women, and men without a college education earn just as much as those with an education. Presenting these facts lends the author an air of evenhandedness.

6. Writing assignment

Classroom Exercise: focus on the argument

Looking around the classroom, do students notice a difference in the number of males compared to the number of females? Have men in the class felt like a minority at any point? Have women noticed a general lack of men on campus? Is there a public policy about male recruitment on campus? What do students think will draw men to campus, and what lengths do they think are appropriate for their school? Is it important to maintain a minimum amount of men at the university? Why? The author points out how this situation parallels affirmative action for minority students, but how might these situations be different?

Katherine S. Mangan   *Bar Association Moves to
Strengthen Diversity
Requirements for Accreditation
of Law Schools*   pp. 931–933

1. According to Mangan, what specific proposal did the ABA make? What details of the proposal are presented here? How do they define the sorts of "concrete steps" that a law school might take to demonstrate its commitment to the requirement? (If you're interested in seeing the actual document that sparked this debate, a version of it is available at <http://abanet.org/legaled/standards/adoptedstandards2006/standards210_212.pdf>.)

Law schools must demonstrate how they are moving toward a goal of diversity. In lieu of actually considering race in admissions, they can be recruiting at historically black colleges, offering specific scholarships, or sponsoring preparatory summer programs.

Why is this proposal controversial?

Some have expressed that this move is a step in the direction of quotas. Others state that underqualified students will be admitted and will find themselves in over their heads.

2. What objections does Professor David E. Bernstein raise to the ABA proposal? How does John A. Sebert, the Association's consultant on legal education, seek to rebut these criticisms?

Bernstein claims that these recommendations work against laws preventing racial preference and that the ABA is pushing racial quotas. Sebert claims that the ABA merely wants to see proof that the schools are seeking qualified minority applicants.

Based on the information given in this article, do Bernstein's criticisms seem well founded? Why or why not? How effective do you find Sebert's replies?

Answers will vary.

3. What arguments might be made in favor of requiring law schools (or professional schools like business schools, engineering schools, or medical schools) to demonstrate that they've taken explicit and concrete steps to achieve an ethnically diverse student body?

If schools have to prove that they are making an effort to recruit minorities, they will take the endeavor more seriously and may find qualified applicants who would not otherwise have applied to the programs.

What arguments might be made against such a requirement?

If schools may have their own "not concrete" ways of recruiting minorities or already have a high number of minority students, the ABA requirements would put an unnecessary burden on them. The money and effort spent on this endeavor might take resources away from other programs at those schools.

4. One way to analyze debates about any sort of affirmative action is to see them as an effort to balance two very different kinds of things. On the one hand, there's the reality of a limited number of places; programs and schools can accommodate only a certain number of students, and for each student who's admitted, some other won't be. On the other hand, there's often a desire to achieve a certain social goal, whether it's ensuring a certain percentage of students from a particular group (for example, males in contrast to females, as detailed in the previous selection) or correcting past injustices (because members of certain groups weren't permitted to enroll, or to enrol in large numbers, or because something about their life history—or the experience of the group of which they're members—has made it difficult for them to be admitted). Which aspects of such arguments are definitional? Causal? Evaluative? Geared to making proposals?

Arguments about affirmative action are definition in that one must delineate who benefits, what qualifies them, and why it is necessary. They become causal when defining the reasons for a lack of certain kinds of students in higher education, and the arguments become evaluative when inspecting specific programs and current practices. Affirmative action initiatives are proposals to make a specific effort to attract particular groups of people into a school, job, or other institution.

5. Writing assignment

The questions at the end of this selection address the advantages and disadvantages of diversity referenda. Reflecting on the evidence presented in this article, students should be able to make suggestions for what they see as acceptable "concrete steps" toward minority recruitment. If students feel that such steps are unnecessary or inappropriate, have them write an opinion piece explaining their position.

Making a Visual Argument: Cartoonists Take On Affirmative Action

Mike Lester *It's GOT to Be the Shoes*

Dennis Draughon *Supreme Irony*

Mike Thompson *Daniel Lives on Detroit's Eastside . . .*

Signe Wilkinson *Admissions*

Dean Camp *Pricey*   pp. 934–938

1. Briefly summarize the argument being made by each cartoon.

   Lester's argument is that racial preferences allow minorities who are not prepared or perhaps qualified to enter college. The Draughon cartoon can have at least two readings: the irony that a nondiverse Supreme Court makes decisions about diversity issues and the irony that many feel that Clarence Thomas is not qualified to be on the Supreme Court and was appointed simply to fill the seat vacated by another African American, the great jurist Thurgood Marshall. Thompson argues that affirmative action helps those who have followed a difficult road to college. Wilkinson argues that many students who receive preferential treatment are not minorities. Camp suggests that wealthier students have the advantage of tutoring and other preparatory programs that others do not have access to.

   Which do you find most effective? Least effective? Why?

   Answers will vary.

2. In what ways do the cartoons by Mike Lester and Dennis Draughon mock the Supreme Court?

Lester uses a clown-judge to claim that the Court is acting ridiculously to allow "unprepared students" into college through racial preference, while Draughon focuses on Justice Clarence Thomas as a member of a minority on the Court.

How does Lester's cartoon use gender and gender stereotypes humorously? How might Sarah Karnasiewicz, author of "The Campus Crusade for Guys," respond to this cartoon?

Boys often develop more slowly than girls, and recently it has been argued that men are not as prepared for college as women are. Karnasiewicz would probably point out that regarding preferences for men, the cartoon is right. It might not be a case of men needing help to get into college but of men choosing other paths.

How does each of these cartoons use irony?

Irony can be seen, respectively, as a white male enters college ahead of a female based on the precedent of racial preferences, a minority in a largely homogeneous group ponders diversity, a minority student who faces difficult odds is accused of being given too many breaks because he enters college through affirmative action, a minority is accused of bumping out a college applicant when there are four other students who might deserve to be there even less, and a white male entering college ahead of others because of preparatory services that he paid for.

3. In what ways do the cartoons by Mike Thompson and Signe Wilkinson make similar arguments? How do their arguments differ?

Both point out that people are often quick to claim that minorities have stolen a spot in school from a better-educated student without stopping to ponder the other circumstances involved. They differ in that the first addresses the reasoning behind affirmative action, while the other points out that privileged persons have long received special consideration for admission.

4. How can the cartoon by Dean Camp be read as relevant to debates about affirmative action?

This cartoon can be seen as a rebuttal to the argument that minorities get all the breaks. Camp reminds the reader that students who come from high-income families (often non-minorities) have more access to courses and coaching to prepare them to compete for college admissions.

5. Writing assignment

Classroom Exercise: focus on the argument

These cartoons represent at least two different views on affirmative action. Have students choose a cartoon that they do not agree with and write a response to the artist. Encourage students to evaluate the cartoon and offer as many insights as they can about the image, text, ethos, and validity of the argument.

Frederick M. Hess   *Schools of Reeducation?*   pp. 939–941

1. What is Frederick Hess's argument in this essay? What practices is he critiquing? How does he do so? Why?

   Hess argues that teachers need not hold specific values to be effective and that therefore colleges should not be policing the values of their students. He is critiquing the practice of monitoring student values and dispositions that has been practiced at some schools of education. He claims that the university should focus on training teachers to teach.

   In what ways is this essay an argument about diversity?

   Hess's argument can be seen as an argument to maintain the diversity of opinion among teachers. If all teachers are trained to subscribe to a specific set of values, there may be a loss of innovation and experience in the classroom.

2. How would you characterize the tone of Hess's argument?

   The tone in the article is one of exasperation.

   What evidence can you give to show that he wishes to be critical? What evidence can you give to show that he simultaneously wishes to be reasonable?

   Hess criticizes the mission statements of schools that seek to instill specific values in their students. At the same time,

the author states that he sympathizes with the good intentions at the root of such statements.

3. In paragraph 4, Hess claims, "The relevance of these skills [namely, an understanding of the complexities of race, power, gender, class, sexual orientation, and privilege in American society] to teaching algebra or the second grade is, at minimum, debatable." If you accept Hess's position, what arguments might each side give for the relevance or irrelevance of such skills in teaching?

On one hand, teaching is a service that focuses on imparting information about certain subject areas to students and does not rely on a teacher's warmheartedness or charm. On the other, teachers who physically punish students or hold prejudices against certain races, classes, or family units may interfere with the learning of some or all of their students.

Which set of arguments do you find more persuasive? Why?

Answers will vary.

4. Hess chooses his examples effectively. Choose two of his examples, explaining why they're ideally suited to support his claims.

Answers will vary.

5. Writing assignment

Classroom Exercise: focus on the argument

Have students consider the examples that are presented in this evidence for Hess's claim. How do they react to the academic situations that he explains and the institutional responses to the situations? Are the situations obvious abuses of power, or could they be more complicated? How might an institution balance its need to defend freedom of speech with its need to protect students and the integrity of the school?

David Horowitz   *In Defense of Intellectual Diversity*   pp. 942–948

1. What argument(s) is David Horowitz making?

Horowitz is arguing that those with conservative views are being penalized on college campuses and are in need of a bill of rights to protects them.

How valid do you find them? Why?

Answers will vary.

2. How does Horowitz characterize the recent history of higher education in America in paragraphs 4–5 and 10? Pay special attention to his word choices, for example, "restore academic values" in paragraph 10.

The author states that institutions of higher education have increasingly been catering to politically correct agendas instead of focusing on education.

How do they give you insight into his understanding of the history of higher education and the readers he's invoking? What evidence does he provide for his claims?

The reader is able to understand that Horowitz does not believe that political views belong in the classroom. His invoked reader is someone who might have already heard negative things about the Academic Bill of Rights. His tone is that of someone defending themselves. The author offers evidence in the form of incidents that occurred at Duke University and the University of North Carolina at Chapel Hill.

3. Horowtiz is critical of professors who discuss "controversial matter on the war in Iraq or the Bush White House in a class whose subject matter is not the war in Iraq, or international relations, or presidential administrations," arguing that the "intrusion of such subject matter, in which the professor has no academic expertise, is a breach of professional responsibility and a violation of a student's academic rights" (paragraph 19). From Horowitz's perspective, should the arguments in Chapters 21 through 28 of this textbook be seen as breaches of the authors' professional responsibility or a violation of your academic rights? Why or why not? By what criteria can such decisions be made?

Answers will vary.

4. In paragraph 8, Horowitz distinguishes between "fostering" and "mandating." Is the distinction a valid one?

Answers will vary.

How does the dispute he describes here compare with the dispute over the American Bar Association's proposal to strengthen diversity requirements for accreditation? (See the news article by Katherine S. Mangan on p. 931.)

The proposals are similar in that both would like universities to be required to take measures to ensure diversity. Both proposals are also hotly contested.

5. Writing assignment

Classroom Exercise: focus on the argument

Have students ever had a difficulty with a professor who penalized them purely for their opinion? Do students think that a student bill of rights would protect them in these cases? Even with an explanation of rights, how do people decide whether a professor is inappropriately pushing political rhetoric versus objectively evaluating a piece of literature that addresses a topic about which they feel strongly? Who should be the arbiter in such a situation? What should constitute proof?

David Horowitz   *Academic Bill of Rights*   pp. 949–952

1. How and why are such statements of principle implicitly and explicitly simultaneously definition arguments and proposal arguments?

   A statement of rights such as this one defines a series of missions or rights associated with an institution. The implication is that the institution will actively ensure that each goal is met and that each right is protected.

2. The eight points listed at the end of this document are said to define the principles in question. Why might there be such a focus on "political or religious beliefs"?

   Horowitz is particularly concerned that professors with liberal agendas are indoctrinating students in their classrooms.

   How would the document be different if only one of these categories were listed? Why or why not?

   Religion and politics represent different parts of American life around which strong personal opinions are wrapped. Leaving out one would make the statement appear to directly attack the other.

3. In the eight points, the humanities and social sciences are treated differently from other branches of intellectual endeavor. Why?

The humanities and social sciences are open to subjective interpretation of some issues. Horowitz sees them as areas of study where conservative views are not well accepted.

Could similar arguments be made for the sciences, for example, in light of recent discussion of intelligent design? Why or why not?

Some could argue that it would be unethical and prejudicial to exclude from the university setting a professor whose research sought to support topics like intelligent design.

4. This document leaves certain key notions unspecified or undefined—for example, "where appropriate" in principle 4, "indoctrination" in principle 5, "and intellectual pluralism," in principle 6. Are there advantages to this situation? Disadvantages? What might they be? Why?

Including some unspecified or undefined items allows them to be interpreted in specific situations. This can be an advantage if the plaintiff and those in power share a definition but could be a disadvantage if there is not a consensus among those involved in a specific situation.

5. Writing assignment

Classroom Exercise: focus on rhetoric

Students should review the Academic Bill of Rights and consider what makes this document a bill of rights rather than a manifesto or a list. Compare the style of Horowitz's document to the Bill of Rights in the U.S. Constitution. Are there similarities? What are the stylistic differences? Have students create an outline of what a bill of rights looks like.

Stanley Fish *"Intellectual Diversity": The Trojan Horse of a Dark Design* pp. 953–959

1. What is Stanley Fish's attitude toward the Academic Bill of Rights and the notion of intellectual diversity?

Fish states that the Academic Bill of Rights is a mistake that will politicize academia even more. He argues that while

professors should not preach their ideologies in class, there should be no mandate to spend equal time in class on theories or methodologies other than their own.

Which issues do Fish and David Horowitz, author of the Academic Bill of Rights, agree about? Which issues do they disagree about? Why?

Both authors agree that students should be able to learn in an environment that is not made hostile by politics or religion. They disagree about the level of "diverse opinions" that should be presented on campus and the level of formal oversight that should exist to promote such diversity.

2. Fish argues that if one agrees that "the pursuit of truth is the cardinal value of the academy," then one must reject the notion of intellectual diversity (paragraph 13). What arguments does he offer for this position?

Fish states that truths are not infallible but that this doesn't mean they must constantly be attacked.

Do you agree or disagree? Why?

Answers will vary.

3. Fish likewise rejects the idea that the job of higher education is to produce "creative individuals" and help students become "productive citizens." What are his arguments for this position?

Fish argues that higher education exists to train students in academics. While some character building might happen as a result of that education, he claims that it is not the responsibility of the institution.

Do you agree or disagree? Why?

Answers will vary.

4. In paragraphs 16–23, Fish contends that despite Horowitz's claims to the contrary, his goal is to "hoist the left by its own petard." What evidence does Fish provide for his claims?

The author points out phrases like "intellectual diversity" and "political correctness" have been appropriated by the right.

How do these claims compare with Horowitz's comments in his essay, "In Defense of Intellectual Diversity"?

Horowitz claims that he is not plotting against the left and that he hopes that the left will embrace his Academic Bill of Rights to protect all students.

5. In paragraph 24, Fish argues that the notion of balance is an unworthy academic goal. What does he mean here?

Here Fish uses the notion of balance to mean giving equal attention to all possible theories on a matter.

Should the idea of balance mean that all possible positions are represented as being of equal value? Should it have some other meaning? Is it, as Fish contends, in contrast to Horowitz, not a useful goal in the pursuit of knowledge or truth?

Answers will vary.

6. Throughout this book, we've argued that images are arguments. Let's consider specifically the photo of Dr. Lynne Cheney that appears near the end of this selection. As the caption notes, it shows Cheney campaigning with her husband, the vice president. We can imagine some readers criticizing us for using a photo of Cheney in which she is represented as acting on behalf of her husband rather than being represented in terms of her own professional achievements. Why might such readers be critical? Others might praise us for using this photo. What might their reasoning be?

The reference in the essay is to Lynne Cheney herself and her political views. A photo of her with her husband might be criticized as creating an image of her as political wife rather than as an academic and political activist in her own right. Others might counter that she has become famous through her role as the wife of the vice president and is most recognized in this role.

What is your opinion about the choice of this photo? What values lead you to your conclusions?

Answers may vary.

7. Writing assignment

Classroom Exercise: focus on the argument

In what way do Fish's predictions about the future of higher education with an Academic Bill of Rights parallel Robert O'Harrow's argument as reviewed by Kakutani? Can students make any Orwellian
connections? On the other hand, does Fish's argument approximate a
"slippery slope" fallacy? Why or why not?

Michael J. Ellis   *Once More unto the Breach*   pp. 960–964

1. What position does Michael Ellis take with respect to "intellectual
   diversity"?

   **Ellis is a conservative who is aware of the low numbers of
   conservative professors but who does not agree that an Academic Bill of Rights should be enacted to police the situation.**

   What upsets him most about "the disproportionate percentage of
   professors who subscribe to liberal or 'progressive' ideologies"
   (paragraph 7)?

   **Conservative students are able to learn much from liberal
   professors, but liberal students are never challenged in
   their beliefs.**

   In contrast to Horowitz, what suggestion does he offer to fellow
   conservatives who might be concerned about the alleged liberal
   bias of professors?

   **Ellis suggests that conservatives should develop strong re-
   search strands of their own and speak up about their findings.**

2. How does Ellis use humor throughout his argument? How does
   humor contribute to his ethos as a writer?

   **Elllis pokes fun at some conservative stereotypes and exag-
   gerates the fears about liberal campuses in an effort to
   bring levity to the conversation. His humor helps build an
   ethos of balance, credibility, and evenhandedness.**

3. What sorts of knowledge does Ellis expect his readers to have?
   What sorts of values? In other words, who are his invoked readers?

The readers invoked in this piece are fellow students at Dartmouth College who know the professors mentioned and the state of liberal and conservative politics at the school.

4. What sorts of evidence does Ellis use in the opening paragraphs to support his argument that liberal faculty have undue influence on campuses?

   Ellis uses examples such as college visits from controversial liberal figures, college outrage at politically incorrect speeches, and strong resistance to conservative trustee campaigns to support his argument that liberal bias is building at universities.

   Why might he have arranged his argument as he did? For example, if he had reordered the information, would his argument have been more or less effective? Why? (For a discussion of kinds of evidence, see Chapter 16.)

   The examples for support begin with the most egregious example, and the following examples are each less well known than the previous. This way, the latter examples are included in the same category as the first. The statistics that follow the section mean nothing on their own but serve as a support for the concrete example presented in paragraph 2.

5. Writing assignment

Classroom Exercise: focus on the argument

Ellis takes an unusual approach by suggesting that the real losers in a liberal academy are the liberal students who never learn about alternative views. How convincing do students find his argument? How does it add to his ethos as a commentator? This essay is taken from an alternative conservative campus newspaper. Is this the kind of writing that students would expect from a conservative paper? From a student writer? Why or why not? Have students write a letter to the editor of the paper remarking on this piece. Remind students to focus on brevity, clarity, and style of argumentation.

Ann Marie B. Bahr   *The Right to Tell the Truth* pp. 965–968

1. What is Ann Marie Bahr's position on intellectual diversity? How does she use her own experience to support her position?

   Bahr states that the push for diversity results in the censorship of teachers who do not stay within the comfort zone of students' beliefs. Her own experience serves as an example of how students feel free to reject what they do not want to hear.

   How effectively does she do so?

   Answers will vary.

2. How does Bahr characterize herself? In other words, what do you, as a reader, know about her values and commitments? How does this knowledge influence the ethos Bahr is able to create?

   Bahr considers herself a conservative scholar who values academic debate. She creates an ethos of frustration, but her description of her beliefs and teaching style helps her argument appear sincere and reasonable.

3. What might Bahr mean when she writes, "I now suspect that the objective, scholarly tone of the books upset my students" (paragraph 4)? What specifically might she mean by "objective" and "scholarly"? Why might her students have wanted or expected some other sort of book?

   Bahr implies that students would prefer to read a work that was partisan and aligned with their own views. She considers works based on fact, unbiased by personal opinion or prejudice, to be objective. A scholarly work is one that consciously situates itself within the academic and historical framework of a particular discipline. If her students were looking to reinforce what they already felt about the topic, they may have wanted or expected a different reading list for the course.

4. What should our response be when works accepted as sound scholarship of the sort mentioned in paragraph 3 of this essay present a less than flattering picture of a group of which we are a member or one for which we have some empathy?

   Answers will vary.

5. Because this essay appeared in the *Chronicle of Higher Education*, we can assume that Bahr's intended readers are professors and administrators at colleges and universities. Thus, throughout

the essay, Bahr is talking about — not to — students when she makes such claims as "The problem is that students do not have the academic maturity to know how to use [Horowitz's "Academic Bill of Rights"] (paragraph 14) and "members of the public and students . . . cannot judge whether I am teaching according to the best standards of the discipline" (paragraph 16). How do you respond to such claims? Why? What sorts of things are students capable of judging? With respect to the sorts of topics covered in college and university courses, is Bahr correct in claiming that there are certain things students (and the general public) are incapable of judging? If so, what would those things be?

Answers will vary.

6. Writing assignment

Classroom Exercise: focus on the argument

How does Bahr's experience perhaps differ from that of Azar Nafisi's "Mysterious Connections That Link Us Together" (Chapter 26)? What might have made Nafisi's students debate with her and later support her while Bahr's students stopped coming to class and later rejected her evaluation of a book that they read. Could there be more to each situation that can be evaluated in the stories as told by the authors? What advice would students offer Bahr for handling next semester's class?

John Tierney *Where Cronies Dwell* pp. 969–971

1. Tierney discusses another aspect of the intellectual diversity controversy — "the stories that . . . no one thinks to do" (paragraph 6). Why does he feel this issue is a matter of some importance?

Tierney's point here is that our ideological leanings affect the choices that we make in research and journalism.

Do you agree or disagree? Why?

Answers will vary.

2. Tierney contends there's bias in hiring in what he terms the "mainstream" publications (paragraphs 10–11). What's the nature of this bias? How is it perpetuated, according to Tierney?

The author claims that people who work at conservative papers or blogs are in jeopardy of not being hired later at mainstream papers.

3. In paragraph 12, Tierney offers a qualification to his argument: "I'm not suggesting that journalism or law schools should be forced to have ideological balance on their faculties—this is one of those many problems that doesn't require a solution by government." How does qualifying his position strengthen Tierney's argument? Why is it important for him to mention this situation as a problem government doesn't need to help solve, given the ethos he creates for himself and the position he has taken on this issue?

By taking a stand against government intervention in liberal journalism, Tierney stays true to his argument that conservatives do not want government interference where it is not needed. This position actually aligns Tierney with many liberals and moderates who would not want to see official oversight on the issue. By joining that consensus for a moment, Tierney shows himself as a rational debater who is confident in his argument.

4. As do all the writers in this chapter, Tierney makes causal claims, among others. What's the exact nature of his causal argument(s)? In other words, for Tierney, what specific causes yield which specific results? (For a discussion of causal arguments, see Chapter 10.)

Tierney argues that the growth of liberal power in media has changed the kinds of stories that make it into the news and has forced conservative journalists to seek other fields or alternative news sources.

5. Tierney cites David Horowitz's studies of the political affiliation of professors in journalism and law schools, and Tierney, like many, finds these results troubling. Why, in your opinion, is the focus on these fields, rather than, say, engineering or biology?

Answers will vary.

6. Writing assignment

Classroom Exercise: focus on the argument

Tierney is making the general argument that a liberal majority is skewing academia and journalism among other institutions. Both are common accusations in today's conservative publications. What makes Tierney's explanation different? Have students respond to this article in the form of a letter to the editor and later compare these letters to the responses in the next selection.

New York Times Letters *Through the Prism of Left and Right: Responses to John Tierney's "Where Cronies Dwell"* pp. 972–975

1. Briefly, summarize the argument each of these letters to the editor makes.

   The letters argue, respectively, that conservatives aren't looking for academic and journalistic jobs, that like-minded people are drawn to similar careers, that conservatives are not interested in academia, that the preponderance of liberals is academia is not by itself evidence of cronyism, that liberals working in academia and journalism leave room for conservatives to work in more lucrative careers, that conservatives look for better-paying careers outside academia, and that if academia paid better, there would be more conservative applicants.

   Which letter do you find most effective in making its point and doing so memorably? Why? Which do you find least effective in doing so?

   Answers will vary.

2. Which letter is most in line with your own response to Tierney's column "Where Cronies Dwell"? Which is least in line? To what extent does your reply to this question correspond to your reply to question 1? Should you be concerned if it does? If it doesn't? Is it possible to separate one's own commitments to or stance about an issue from one's evaluations of arguments about that issue?

   Answers will vary.

3. Which letters present actual criticism of the arguments Tierney made, and which are more general critiques of the broader position he takes?

   All of the letters represent general critiques of the position.

   Focusing on those that criticize specific arguments made by Tierney, make a list of the aspects of his column these letter writers objected to.

   The letter writers object to Tierney's accusation of cronyism and anticonservative prejudice in hiring.

4. If you take these letters to be successful—they did manage to get published, after all—what are the criteria for a successful letter to the editor of the *New York Times?*

   Successful letters are short, remain on topic, and make one or two major points. The writers are well spoken and in this case not conservative.

5. The *Times*, like many newspapers, sometimes provides one sentence of information about who a letter writer is. How does such information—or its absence—likely influence readers' evaluations of the letter? Of the letter writer?

   The brief biographical lines tell readers where the writers are from and occasionally what their profession is. Readers can then factor in a writer's region and occupation as they determine what the writer might have at stake in his or her argument.

6. Writing assignment

Classroom Exercise: focus on the world

Students now have written a few letters to an editor and have read several examples, so they should have a good idea of what the genre entails. Letters are addressed to the editor, generally directed to the author of a previous piece, and written with the full knowledge that publication is a possibility. How does maintaining these three audiences in mind affect the style and tone of these letters? How might the letters to the editor differ across cultures? (Can any international students or students who read foreign papers speak to this?)

Walter Benn Michaels   *Diversity's False Solace* pp. 976–978

1. Why does Walter Benn Michaels contend that diversity offers a "false solace" at best? What, in his opinion, is the real issue American society needs to confront?

   Michaels argues that focusing on racial diversity leads us to forget that most students in college come from economically privileged families. He claims that we should confront the fact that poor students are not prepared to go to college.

How, for him, does arguing about ethnic diversity simultaneously insulate Americans from seeing the real issue while preventing them from dealing with it?

The task of cultural diversity keeps people from realizing that the poor are not at college. A focus on cultural diversity leads us to ignore the cultural privilege of birth and the financial privilege of birth of many college students.

2. For what reasons does Michaels argue that the notions of culture and cultural difference are comforting ones? And why, in his opinion, is race such an unpleasant one for Americans?

Michaels does not mention why he thinks that people prefer to talk about culture rather than race. The focus on culture rather than race probably stems from an attempt to move away from a historically shameful situation in American history and to focus on celebrating the traditions and practices of groups based on their heritage.

3. How does Michaels fit his observations about diversity into the American political landscape, recasting it in terms of the liberal left and the conservative right?

If the left is busy worrying about cultural diversity, then it does not have time to challenge conservatives about helping the poor.

4. What sort of ethos does Michaels create for himself in this essay?

Michaels presents himself as a concerned academic who is critical of current admissions criteria.

What sorts of appeals does he use—ethical appeals, emotional appeals, logical appeals? How do they contribute to the tone of the essay and the ethos Michaels creates for himself?

Michaels presents logical appeals to support his argument. With statistics and student opinion, he challenges the reader to imagine a situation where the poor were represented proportionately in college.

5. Writing assignment

Michaels makes the point that liberals who focus on diversity are too busy to argue with conservatives about helping the poor. How do students think that Michaels might label himself in this dichotomy that he has created? What evidence supports this conclusion? Do students agree that they or their college administrators prefer to talk about culture rather than race? Why or why not? Is either topic a subject that they are comfortable with? How do they feel about discussing class? Socioeconomic position?

Wrap-up Exercises for Constructing Arguments about "Diversity on Campus"

These final assignments are provided as an opportunity to reflect on the readings as a whole and to construct arguments based on what students have taken away from the selections. Question 3 is appropriate for use as an in-class essay.

1. Investigate the diversity mission at your institution by looking at various Web sites and statistics that may be published. Then look for any news items over the years that chronicle your school's history of minority inclusion. Write an essay in which you evaluate the progress or lack of progress that you see in the school's definition of diversity and its handling of diversity.

2. Interview five to ten students at your institution about their views of the liberal or conservative nature of the school. Concentrate on interviewing individuals who probably hold different political ideals than your own to familiarize yourself with that point of view with regard to your own environment. Find out how they view the institution as a whole, other students, professors, the level of ideology in the classroom, and even their ideas about remedying any problems that they see. Use what you learn to write an essay in which you evaluate their claims and present what you understand to be happening on campus.

3. Write an essay about how you would increase the cultural diversity of a student body or the ideological diversity of a faculty if you were the head of a committee charged with presenting possible tools for increasing diversity without using affirmative action. Alternatively, construct an argument for affirmative action as the best way to increase either student or faculty diversity.

CHAPTER 28

Why Do They Love Us?
Why Do They Hate Us?

Have you traveled outside the United States or watched a foreign television program or news report and been surprised by local opinions about Americans? Did you find the characterizations fair or unfair? Because we export so much more media than we import, many Americans remain unaware of the stereotypes and assumptions about Americans that exist beyond our borders. The war on terrorism has brought more of this to light, but it is still not a major topic of conversation for Americans. This new awareness has caused Americans to confront the preconceived notions that we have of other people — including Arabs, Arab Americans, and Muslims in general. During a time when America's actions abroad are being watched closely, these readings invite us to ponder how each of us is involved with shaping the perception of the United States. This introspection prompts us to address questions such as the following:

- How concerned should Americans be about their reputation abroad? How much do media stereotypes or general ill will among a citizenry affect international relations at the political level?
- What stereotypes do the U.S. media perpetuate about other countries? How might film and TV portrayals of other nationalities affect our general opinions of those people?

Hannah Fairfield *America: Not Their First Choice* pp. 983–985

1. What's your response to this selection? Surprise? Amazement? Anger? Agreement? Why? How do you think most Americans would respond to these data? Why?

Answers will vary.

2. Evaluate this selection as a visual argument. How clear and easy to follow is it? What principle, if any, accounts for the ordering of countries in the column on the left? In the rows across the top?

Answers will vary.

What principle, if any, accounts for the relative size of the circles representing responses? The shading of circles?

Each circle's size represents the relative size of the percentage with which it is labeled. The shaded circles represent the most popular answer for that country.

3. Try to divide the countries in the left column into subgroups based on some characteristic they share—for example, Northern European countries, countries with large Muslim populations, traditional friends or allies of the United States, countries that have opposed the United States and that the United States has opposed at some time since World War II, and so on. Do any patterns in responses begin to emerge once you examine these subgroups?

Countries with large Muslim populations tended to choose countries outside the most popular four. They chose France (most likely if they are French speakers), Japan, China, and the United Arab Emirates. Russia and Turkey both rated Germany the highest. The Eastern European countries leaned toward three English-speaking countries — the United States, Canada, and Britain.

4. Writing assignment

5. Writing assignment

Classroom Exercise: focus on rhetoric

Americans often warn that our borders are rupturing from the weight of immigrants who are waiting to enter the country. How does this visual challenge that contention or at least put it in a new perspective? Where do students think that Americans would prefer to start over if they could? What circumstances do students think lead Americans to choose the locations that expatriates favor when they leave the United States? Have students create a tourism ad that highlights a specific area of the world in a way that might attract Americans. They can target retirees, college students, or even young professionals. You can focus the task, or you can alow students to choose how to combine visual and text.

Richard Bernstein   *The Days After:*
                        The View from Abroad   pp. 986–989

1. What is Richard Bernstein's argument? What causes does he give in response to his short question, "Why?" (paragraph 4)?

    Bernstein argues that public opinion abroad after Hurricane Katrina was not as sympathetic for the United States as Americans might have expected. His answer to "Why?" is that people in other countries were disappointed that the government of a wealthy country was not ready to handle this emergency.

2. According to Bernstein, what vision of Americans did Europeans have at the time he wrote the column? What might Europeans mean by "solidarity" (paragraph 14)?

    The author claims that Europeans felt sympathy for those involved in the hurricane but considered the inadequate rescue response to be symptomatic of a government that ignores the poor. Here, a lack of solidarity means the absence of a spirit of oneness and mutual support among Americans.

3. How does Bernstein see the responses of Europeans to Hurricane Katrina as evidence that a people's responses to others' tragedies say much about how they see themselves? (Examine paragraph 8, for example.) Were the Europeans merely being smug, or might other things have been going on? In other words, what might Europeans' response to Katrina tell us about their own worst fears?

    Europeans would like to believe that their countries are prepared for predicted disasters such as hurricanes. The disorganized American response to the hurricane might have led Europeans to wonder whether such a thing could happen to them. If America couldn't handle it, could their own hometowns?

4. What's your response to this "view from abroad"? How often are you exposed to views from abroad—that is, to responses to events in the United States or to reactions to the behavior of the United States

as reported by foreign news media rather than American media? Are there disadvantages to the fact that few Americans seem to be exposed to such views? Many Web sites created in other countries and languages are available in English-language versions. Will this fact likely increase Americans' exposure to views from abroad? Should it? What might the consequences of such exposure be?

Answers will vary.

5. Writing assignment

Classroom Exercise: focus on the world

The United States is often held to higher standards of performance in financial and social justice situations than are other countries. How might America's own actions and declarations have led to such a harsh judgment? How would students as Americans (or residents or visiting students) characterize the government's response to Hurricane Katrina? Could we have been more prepared? Was the problem a series of bad judgments or overwhelmed resources? Even if students do not agree, can they empathize with the criticism from abroad? Do students think that the criticism stems from this disaster in particular or from a history of behavior? Will the United States always be under scrutiny as long as it remains the world's most powerful country?

Waleed Ziad   *Jihad's Fresh Face*   pp. 990–994

1. What are Waleed Ziad's proposals for dealing with "jihad's fresh face," or what he terms neo-fundamentalism?

   Ziad recommends providing aid to Muslim groups that provide services that their governments do not offer to better the lives of those who would otherwise see jihad as the answer to their difficulties.

   What particular problems do his proposals seek to redress? What caused these problems in the first place?

   His proposal addresses women's rights, small business development, and a free market. These rights and activities are ignored or not allowed under the autocratic rulers that control some parts of the world.

2. Ziad's selection represents a complete proposal argument. It contains definitional arguments, causal arguments, and evaluative ar-

guments, and, based on these elements, it offers a proposal. Find the relevant sections of the selection that represent each kind of argument.

Definitional argument: Ziad opens with a definition of the American view of jihad followed by his definition of neo-fundamentalists. Causal argument: The next section describes the political climate that led to neo-fundamentalism. Evaluative argument: The author describes what he thinks propels the movement and how U.S. reactions play into their continued existence. Proposal: Ziad ends the argument with a suggestion for how to handle aid for Muslim parts of the world more effectively.

3. Why does Ziad include the historical information included in paragraphs 7–14?

Presenting a historical context for different eras of fundamentalism helps the reader to understand Ziad's argument and lends support to his conclusions.

Is such information new to you? Given the discussion of Islamic neo-fundamentalism since the events of September 11, 2001, why, in your opinion, has historical information like that given here generally been absent from public discussion?

Answers will vary.

How does this absence encourage Americans and Westerners more generally to believe that Islam and Muslim societies are frozen in time, somewhere in the distant past?

Without information about the evolution of Islam and Muslim political systems and fundamental movements, outsiders might see Muslim societies as underdeveloped and static.

4. As noted in a marginal gloss, the neoconservatives argue that perhaps America's greatest imperative is to spread American-style democracy around the world, replacing repressive rulers, if necessary, with democratically elected governments. According to Ziad, what else should the United States be doing if it has such goals?

Ziad argues that the United States should support Muslim social services and economies to help those communities

make their own decisions about how their governments should change. Such aid would allow people to prosper and then question fundamentalism.

5. Ziad's comments assume that Americans, including American policy-makers, generally distrust anyone or anything associated with Islam. How does he reply to this tendency? Why is his use of the phrase "faith-based" in the article's final paragraph important in this regard?

   The author argues that Americans should not confuse Muslim organizations with fundamentalist actions. His mention of Muslim faith-based organizations echos President Bush's support for American faith-based groups that work under government contracts.

6. What do you understand the argument of the hand-drawn illustration that accompanies this selection to be?

   Answers will vary.

7. Writing assignment

Classroom Exercise: focus on rhetoric

Ziad discusses the history of Islamic fundamentalism to fight the stereotypes that see Islam and the countries where it is practiced as frozen in time. Can students think of other ethnicities that Americans (and perhaps others) often think of as frozen in time? Do these examples represent indigenous communities that are seen as less developed? Do they represent communities that are now "Westernized" but are still romanticized as retaining all of their old ways? How is folk history like this perpetuated? What is the best way to combat these outdated beliefs?

David Rieff   *Their Hearts and Minds?*   pp. 995–998

1. David Rieff's argument is evaluative in several regards. What assumptions held by many Americans and President George W. Bush's administration is Rieff questioning?

   Rieff is questioning the assumption that other countries crave democracy and that democracy is a viable or optimal option for every nation.

What evidence does he provide for the need to question these assumptions? What is Rieff's evaluation of them?

Rieff offers several different kinds of support for his argument. First, he compares the relationship between Islamic fundamentalism and Muslim citizens to the relationship between communism and the citizens it has to convert. Then he emphasizes the Islamic fundamentalists' rejection of modernity and globalization. Finally, he presents Egypt as an example of the difficulties that the United States faces in selling democracy.

What is yours? Why? Why is questioning someone's assumptions often a useful strategy in constructing an argument?

Answers will vary.

2. Rieff compares and contrasts the United States' "war of ideas" against communism and what he terms "jihadism" (paragraphs 6–7). (Comparison—discussing similarities—and contrast—discussing differences—often form part of an evaluative argument.) What similarities does he see? What differences?

Rieff contends that the United States looks at its victory over communism as a model for taking on jihadism, but he points out that jihadism has long had a hold on people because it is based on their religious faith but that communism did not have that advantage. He further notes that communism embraced many modern concepts like education and gender equality but that jihad is antimodernity. Rieff does concede that both jihadism and communism stand against the individual and support mass murder.

How does this section of his argument contribute to his overall argument?

Answers will vary.

3. Examine the visual argument "Foreign Opinions," based on data from the 2005 Pew Global Attitudes Project, which was discussed in the first selection in this chapter. What percentage of the population of each country is Muslim? What's the number of Muslims living in each of the countries listed? (You'll likely need to use the Internet to answer these questions.) Why is this information

useful—or even necessary—in understanding these data? Does this visual argument work to support or contextualize Rieff's claims? Why or why not?

Answers will vary.

How does the photograph of Muslim men prostrating themselves as they participate in Friday communal prayers in Iraq contribute to his argument?

This photo emphasizes the strong religious tradition in Iraq, which supports Rieff's argument that many citizens are practicing Muslims. He further argues that this makes jihadism an attractive movement because it shares many religious beliefs with Islam.

4. Writing assignment

Classroom Exercise: focus on rhetoric

Have students ever stopped to question whether democracy is the best option for other countries? Even if 100 percent of the U.S. population was confident that democracy has been the best thing that ever happened to America, does that mean that it will work in every country? How similar to us does another country have to be to be left alone? At what point does the United States get involved in foreign politics? When another country threatens the United States? When it mistreats its own people? To what degree? What kind of pressure (aid termination, trade embargos, nuclear threats) can change a country like Cuba or Iraq into a democratic nation? Are there other ways to help a people in need or diffuse a tense political relationship?

Making a Visual Argument: How Others See Us

Anipas P. Delotavo Jr.   *Europe Gave Us Shakespeare . . .*

Zaid Omar   *Misconception*

Jibby Yunibandhu   *At Home with the Braves*   pp. 999–1002

1. What is your response to each of these paintings? Is it primarily visceral—a feeling in the gut, emotional, intellectual, or some com-

bination of these? Why, in your opinion? Is one of these categories of response more important? Why or why not?

Answers will vary.

2. Examine the imagery and title of each of the three paintings. How has the artist used them to support his or her argument? With respect to Delotavo's painting, *Europe Gave Us Shakespeare and Beethoven; America Gave Us Jesse James and John Wayne*, pay special attention to the spots on the horse. How do the images of Jesse James and John Wayne relate to contemporary political debates around the world about America's proper role?

Delotavo depicts a cowboy riding over the Middle East. Many have argued that the United States uses a cowboy mentality and cowboy actions to overrule outside opinion and push its will on others.

With respect to Omar's *Misconception*, what conflicting images does he offer of Arabs (and, perhaps, Islam)? What does his work remind us about the importance of perspective?

Omar presents a dove of peace and a bomb of war as two possible images of Arabs. Perspective allows the viewer to see peace or war in the painting.

With respect to Jibby Yunibandhu's *At Home with the Braves*, what historical and visual allusion does she employ to make her argument? What must one know about American history in order to appreciate this painting? What must one know about American culture to appreciate its title?

Yunibandhu paints an immigrant sewing the flag as Betsy Ross once did. This immigrant woman is in "the home of the brave" from the American national anthem. Perhaps her experiences in the United States have made her feel at home.

3. What might Americans learn from these visual arguments about how they're seen around the world?

Americans might learn that they are seen as major participants in globalization. Some feel that Americans are a threat, and others feel that Americans are friends. Few are neutral in how they see us.

What challenges and resources do America, its culture, and its power present to people and nations in an increasingly globalized world as they seek to maintain a sense of identity?

American culture is a threat to the individuality of smaller, less powerful nations. The influence that American culture has in business, politics, and youth popular culture makes it attractive while at the same time overwhelming.

4. Writing assignment

Classroom Exercise: focus on the world

Do students find it ironic that some paintings about globalization focus on America and its international reputation? Students who have grown up in the United States are probably accustomed to living in the "center" of the world, but ask students to imagine what it must be like to have so many products (like food, electronics, hygiene essentials, cars, music, and videos, among others) come from and represent a different country that is bigger and more powerful.

Dinesh D'Souza   *America the Beautiful: What We're Fighting For*   pp. 1003–1014

1. What does Dinesh D'Souza contend America and Americans are "fighting for"? Why, for D'Souza, are these things worth the fight?

   D'Souza claims that America represents a "new way to be human" with all the possibilities for a good life, the "most decent society in existence." He claims that by defending America we join the ranks of all others who have made grave sacrifices, thus making ourselves worthy of her goodness.

   To what extent to you agree with his reasons for fighting and his assessment of the value of these reasons?

   Answers will vary.

2. Throughout his essay, D'Souza uses definitions as part of his argument; for example, he defines the terms "American exceptionalism" (paragraph 1), "American universalism" (paragraph 1), "the reformist or classical liberal response" (paragraph 11), "the fundamentalist argument" (paragraph 12), "Promise Keepers" (para-

graph 19), and "multiculturalists" (paragraph 22). What kind of definitions does he offer for each of these terms? (For a discussion of kinds of definitions, see Chapter 8.)

The definitions that D'Souza offers are operational in nature as they outline the conditions that satisfy each category.

How do these definitional arguments contribute to the essay's major argument?

Answers will vary.

3. After distinguishing between societies that are "self-directed" and those that are "directed by others" (paragraph 26), D'Souza argues in paragraph 28: "the externally directed life that Islamic fundamentalists seek undermines the possibility of virtue." Do you agree or disagree? Why?

Answers will vary.

Although D'Souza is making a specific claim about Islamic fundamentalists, to what extent does his claim apply to all religious fundamentalists who long for a society in which their understanding of God's truth plays a defining role in determining the country's laws and shaping its culture?

This claim could be aimed at any fundamentalist group that sees its own ideology as the only viable option for all people. One example is "Christian" hate groups that preach attacking nonbelievers or that celebrate the tragedies that befall them.

4. Like David Rieff in "Their Hearts and Minds?" D'Souza refers to Vietnam (for example, paragraphs 3 and 25) although he doesn't mention it when he lists specific battles in three wars in the essay's closing paragraph. Why is Vietnam relevant to discussions of the War on Terror? How does D'Souza use his discussion of Vietnam to help support his claim and structure his argument?

In his introductory statements, D'Souza points to Vietnam as a war that the United States lost because it was not sure (or invested in) what its soldiers were fighting for. The author uses this claim as a basis for his argument that must realize what is at stake in the war against terror.

5. Although D'Souza makes very strong claims, he frequently qualifies them and anticipates or acknowledges potential counterarguments to his own. For example, in paragraph 6, D'Souza writes, "The reason that most of us do not think this way now" and "This is not to suggest that Islam's historical abuses are worse than those of the West." In what ways do these rhetorical practices strengthen D'Souza's argument?

By qualifying his statements, the author enhances the reasoned and balanced tone of his essay.

Find other examples of these strategies elsewhere in his essay.

Answers will vary.

6. Near the beginning and end of his essay in paragraphs 2 and 32, respectively, D'Souza uses personification, a kind of figurative language, when he writes about America: "what America does, and what she stands for" and "our willingness to die for her." He doesn't refer to other countries, empires, or cultures as persons—for example, "Israel . . . it" (paragraph 10). Whereas in the past it was quite common to refer to countries, automobiles, and ships in writing by using feminine pronouns, thus personifying them, the practice may strike some readers as quaint and others as sexist today. (For a discussion of biased or slanted language, see Chapter 17.) How does D'Souza's use of personification constitute an emotional appeal?

Personifying America makes it a tangible entity that should be protected like a relative. America as a woman in danger garners more emotion than a land territory or political nation.

Do you find it effective? Why or why not?

Answers will vary.

7. Writing assignment

Classroom Exercise: focus on the world

Ask students what makes the United States "universal," "exceptional," and the "most decent society in existence." Might other nationals differ? What might other countries have to say about America's exceptionalism? With our exceptionalism in mind, are Americans fighting to spread exceptionalism or to maintain our own exceptionalism?

Mark Hertsgaard *The Oblivious Empire* pp. 1015–1027

1. What is the meaning of Mark Hertsgaard's title, "The Oblivious Empire"? How does it summarize his argument?

   The American people are largely oblivious to the U.S. government's actions abroad and to foreign public opinion of the United States. Hertsgaard argues that American obliviousness compounds that indignation abroad.

   Do you agree with his claim that Americans are generally unaware of the role their government's actions have played in world politics? Why or why not? To what extent were you aware of the historical evidence he details in the second section of the essay, 'Why Don't They Tell Us?"? Does it matter if you were? If you weren't? Why or why not?

   Answers will vary.

2. According to Hertsgaard, people from other countries "dislike both how America behaves overseas and its attitude about that behavior" (paragraph 11). How does he and those he cited characterize America's behavior? Its attitude about those actions?

   Hertsgaard is referring to the manipulation of foreign governments and global markets by using financial and military threats. He claims that most Americans are unaware of much of this behavior.

   In the context of the information Hertsgaard provides, do such assessments seem justified or rational? Why or why not?

   Answers will vary.

3. In criticizing the actions of the U.S. government, Hertsgaard cites cases involving both Democratic and Republican administrations. Is he even-handed in this treatment of both parties—that is, is he equally critical (or laudatory) of the behavior of both parties? Why or why not?

   Answers will vary.

4. What kinds of evidence does Hertsgaard rely on in constructing his argument? How does he use evidence effectively?

   Hertsgaard uses historical references, statistics, and quotations from other writings to support his argument. He uses

evidence of all three types to create broad support for each of his arguments.

How successful is his opening narrative based on personal experience? Why?

Answers will vary.

5. Writing assignment

Classroom Exercise: focus on the world

Do students agree that Americans are largely unaware of our reputation outside the United States.? Do students seem themselves as more aware than the previous generation? Is it conservative or liberal to talk about America's oblivious nature? Is it Republican or Democratic?

Thomas L. Friedman   *Revolution Is U.S.*   pp. 1028–1037

1. How does Thomas Friedman use his contrasting definitions of "imperialism" and "global arrogance" to help structure his argument?

   Friedman argues that global arrogance means that the United States does not need to invade other countries physically to spread its influence. He goes on to give examples of America's power abroad that stems from its reputation, popular culture, business activities, and political decisions.

   Writing in 1999, Friedman contends that people around the world are more concerned about our nation's global arrogance than its imperialism. How might America's military presence in Afghanistan and, even more so Iraq subsequent to the events of September 11, 2001, complicate the feelings of citizens of other countries toward the United States, exacerbating already existing anti-Americanism?

   Anger at American arrogance compounds fears and anger about a potential imperialism.

2. Friedman might argue that the question "Why do they hate us?" isn't the question Americans should be asking because it misconstrues the situation. Instead, he argues that globalization, a force much larger than anything America controls, is in the driver's seat (for example, in paragraph 14). From this perspective, every coun-

try has to struggle to survive, and some countries are better equipped to do so than others. For Friedman, what do Americans need to understand about America in the world and why?

Americans need to understand that in many ways Americanization is tied to globalization and that many who resent global influence or modernity resent the United States. Some resent the United States for what it represents, and others resent the actual actions that the United States has taken.

3. Friedman lists a range of possible responses countries can have to the United States and illustrates them. What possible responses does he discuss? Which countries illustrate each?

Russia sought a bailout by the IMF and at the same time complained about American interference. China has avoided the term *globalization* (because of its American implications) in favor of *modernization*. Some countries, like Japan, complain about U.S. power but are happy to enjoy the benefits of U.S. negotiations with other countries. Countries like France and Russia seek to undermine American diplomacy and power abroad.

Which example(s) do you find most memorable? Why?

Answers will vary.

How can this rhetorical strategy be seen as constructing a definitional argument based on examples? (For a discussion of examples and definitional arguments, see Chapter 8.)

Friedman uses the examples to draw out patterns of behavior instead of defining the behavior itself.

4. Friedman cites a conversation with Yuan Ming, one of China's leading experts on the United States, during which she explained why the Chinese government always speaks of "modernization" but never "globalization" (paragraph 10). What does this example reveal about the challenges of cross-cultural communication, even when everyone is speaking the same language?

Words carry different nuances of meaning and represent different ideologies or stances, depending on who is using

them. This is particularly true when communicating cross-culturally. One must be careful about the full meanings and implications of international terms like *globalization*.

5. Friedman likewise reports a conversation with Dominique Moisi, a leading French expert on international affairs, during which she commented that "America has become a mirror of our own doubts. We look at you and see what's missing" (paragraph 17). Moisi was speaking of France when she used "our," but her observation could be shared by thinkers in many other countries. What burden does such a situation place on the United States?

Other countries look to the United States as a model. They see the influence that the United States has and seek to emulate its success. The United States must realize the role that it plays as such a model and consider the responsibilities that go with that.

6. Writing assignment

Classroom Exercise: focus on the world

What sort of influences have other countries had on American culture? Do students listen to music, watch movies, wear clothing, or use products from other countries? Why? Do students think any of these foreign products or ideas have had a tremendous impact on American culture, or changed the way the younger generation thinks about the world? Have students discuss what American culture would be like if foreign products or media were not allowed into the American market or if importation were severely restricted. At what point would we call something American? Have students write an evaluation of this sort of restricted U.S. culture.

Josef Joffe   *The Perils of Soft Power*   pp. 1038–1044

1. Joseph Joffe's argument begins by offering definitions for soft power and hard power and critiquing soft power and its uses. How persuasive do you find his analysis of the situation he describes? Why?

Answers will vary.

2. Joffe has much to say about the cultural elite in European countries — those who care about "high culture" and especially the

classical music, painting, and literature of their own countries' traditions — in contrast to those interested in popular culture, which appeals to the majority of the people, or folk culture, which represents traditional, often rural crafts. Part of his argument is that the European cultural elite dislike American culture and its popularity for several reasons. What are they? Does Joffe believe that the majority of Europeans share the opinions of the cultural elite? Why or why not?

The cultural elite in European countries argue that American art is inferior to European art and that much of American style is built on or stolen from European art. Joffe claims that these opinions are not held by the majority outside the cultural elite because the elite resentment stems mostly from a fear of maintaining their own position in the art world and their disgust at how popular some American exhibits in Europe have been.

3. What proposal does Joffe make to Europeans, including the cultural elite, with respect to "the cultural contest" (paragraph 15)? How would Thomas Friedman, author of "Revolution Is U.S.," respond to such a proposal? Why?

   Joffe suggests that to be competitive Europe will have to borrow back American ideas in art and build on them to create new styles and win back their audience. Friedman would probably predict that such a move would be unlikely for countries like France, Russia, or Japan, which might be too proud to borrow blatantly from the United States.

   What is your response? Why?

   Answers will vary.

4. As is very evident from the glosses for this selection, Joffe's style is laced with allusions to high culture and French words (though he's German). In fact, many of the English words we've glossed were borrowed into English from French or Latin, via French. How do you respond to Joffe's writing style? Is it effective, given his argument? His audience in the *New York Times Sunday Magazine*? Do you think you were among Joffe's intended or invoked readers? Why or why not? Would you expect writing styles — even if one is writing in English — to vary across cultures and countries? Why or why not?

   Answers will vary.

5. Although Joffe doesn't mention the data included in "Cultural Complex" and they were no doubt added by the editors of the *Times*, they support his argument. How?

The data support his argument in that a majority of people responded that they do enjoy American popular culture even while the culture of America is "reviled."

How does the photograph of a movie marquee in Paris add credibility to his claims?

France is famously defensive against American culture, and yet in the photo an American movie poster is looming over an urban square.

6. Writing assignment

Classroom Exercise: focus on the argument

Might those outside the United States feel even more threatened by soft power than by America's political actions abroad? If people willingly chose to embrace globalization or Americanism, why would that be so bad? Shouldn't people have a choice? Such choices are similar to those faced by indigenous groups around the world that are pressured to assimilate at the hands of the cultures that colonize their territories. What does it mean when a culture assimilates into or borrows heavily from another? Can we call it a free and informed decision? Do these minority groups have the luxury of a choice or must they "get on the train"?

Richard Pells   *Is American Culture "American"?*   pp. 1045–1054

1. What is Richard Pells's argument about the sources, nature, and uniqueness of American culture? What reasons and evidence does he give for his claims? Why, for him, is American culture cosmopolitan, rather than imperialistic?

Pells argues that American culture and art are heavily based on ideas borrowed from other nations. As a nation of immigrants, America has much from which to draw. U.S. artists are able to use influences from abroad, reinvent them, and present them again to the world. This is not an imperialistic move but an act of a cosmopolitan citizen that has had varied influences.

2. Although the Web site we found this essay on carries the disclaimer, "The opinions expressed in this article do not necessarily reflect the views or policies of the U.S. government," why might the U.S. Department of State have chosen to include it there? What sort of argument does this essay make to the world about American culture? Why is the disclaimer significant? How is it American?

The State Department may hope that visitors to their site will consider the heritage of American culture and America's role in propelling culture forward. This essay reminds readers that America is great because of the influences from other countries that have shaped it. On the other hand, the government would not want to make a public statement about who has influenced the United States or how much. It is American to have such a disclaimer because Americans believe in offering divergent and interesting opinions for debate.

3. To the extent that Pells's claims are correct, especially his contention that "the influence of immigrants on the United States explains why its culture has been so popular for so long in so many places" (paragraph 4), what implications might his argument have for debates about immigration policies in the United States?

One could use Pells's claims to support an argument for the positive affect of continuing immigrant influences on art and culture in the United States.

4. Pells relies heavily on examples, mentioning the names of painters, art movements, musicians, actors, directors, and films. In so doing, he includes examples from high culture and popular culture. We predict that few readers will have the background knowledge to appreciate and evaluate all of his examples, a fact Pells is surely aware of. What purposes do these examples serve, then? How do they help him turn real readers into invoked readers — perhaps the ultimate task of all writers?

The words that Pells chose to use are examples of America's European history. He probably used these words to drive that thought home to readers.

5. Writing assignment

Do students think that the appeal of American culture is its cosmopolitan nature, or the power that it represents? For example, what makes American movies so popular? The stars? Special effects? Bigger budgets? Better advertising? Or could it be the diversity of style and genera within the American industry? Have each student choose an American product that has strong global appeal and consider what makes it such a strong candidate for wide acceptance. What are its rival products and where are they from? If time permits, have students research the history and popularity of the product.

Michael Medved   *That's Entertainment? Hollywood's Contribution to Anti-Americanism Abroad*   pp. 1055–1069

1. Why, in the opinion of Michael Medved, do people from other countries misunderstand the United States and American culture? Why do they find American cinema appealing? Why do they dislike it?

   Medved argues that American films and television programs send the wrong message about American culture and that those outside the United States judge its character based on the skewed presentations in the movies and on TV. He claims that American films are popular with the masses because watching the violence and decadent behavior makes others feel better about their own countries. On the other hand, they are disgusted by what they see as American culture captured in film.

2. Medved's essay is a proposal argument. What proposals is he making? To whom?

   Medved is proposing that Hollywood and the rest of American media stop producing the kind of content that he thinks embarrasses us overseas. His appeal is aimed at Americans who want to change America's image overseas.

   How might Thomas Friedman, author of "Revolution Is U.S.," and Richard Pells, author of "Is American Culture 'American'?" evaluate them? Why?

   Pells would probably argue that other countries do not like America's predominance in media and that changing the

kinds of films would not solve any problems. Friedman would agree and reiterate that it is not so much American media's message as the preponderance of American media and culture infiltrating abroad that arouses such negative opinions.

What's your evaluation of them?

Answers will vary.

3. Medved closes his argument by referring to values Americans learn in their families, noting "In our families, we find love and learn responsibility and character" (paragraph 36). Do you think he would number among American families the "loving and wholesome relationship . . . between two clean-cut gay male neighbors" mentioned in his discussion of *American Beauty* (paragraph 15). Why or why not? Should he? Why or why not? Would you? Why or why not?

Answers will vary.

4. If all you knew about American women came from American movies or television programs that you had watched, what view would you have of them? How does such a view contrast with the view you in fact have? How does such a contrast support Medved's point? Might it help account for why American women who travel abroad often complain bitterly of being harassed?

Answers will vary.

5. In paragraph 17, Medved employs an interesting rhetorical strategy when he cites research to support claims he has made in an earlier book he had written. How do you respond to such a strategy and Medved's use of it? Does it contribute to his ethos in a positive or negative way? Why?

Answers will vary.

Why might it be risky to cite research in support of one's own earlier claims?

Quoting research that supports an earlier claim implies that at the time the claim was made it was not based on research. Medved runs the risk of appearing like someone whose claims are not grounded in empirical or reliable data.

7. Writing assignment

Have students choose a movie or TV series from another country that has been broadcast on American television and consider the way in which it portrays the people of that country. Is it a satire? A drama? A soap opera? A thriller? A game show? A comedy? Do the students imagine that the characters presented in the work are true examples of people in the country of origin? Do they represent the most populous class of the country? Do they represent the most conservative, religious, or traditional people of the country? Would watching and noting the social commentary and lifestyle of those in the film or show be good training for a visit to that country? Would it give insight into how "normal people" in that country live, work, and view the world?

Making a Visual Argument: Exporting America

Les Stone   *Advertisement for Metropolitan Life Insurance in Taipei*

China Features/Corbis Sygma   *Poster for the Film* Titanic *in Peking*

Tatiana Markow   *McDonald's in Shanghai*

Koren Ziv   *Nike in Jerusalem*

Haruyoshi Yamaguchi   *Mother and Children at DisneySea, the Disney Theme Park in Japan*

John Van Hasselt   *Advertising Budweiser as Capitalism Comes to China*

John Van Hasselt   *Selling Coke and Pepsi in India*

Mohsen Shandiz   *Coca-Cola and Marlboro in Iran*   pp. 1070–1078

1. Based on these photographs, which aspects of American culture have been exported around the world, especially to developing nations?

American products and media have been imported around the world. Fast food, beer, and soda from the United States have traveled even to poor countries.

Are these aspects of American culture you're proud of? Why or why not?

Answers will vary.

2. How might the authors whose work is represented in this chapter respond to these photos? Would they be encouraged, discouraged, or both? Why?

Answers will vary.

3. Can the artifacts represented here symbolize the spread of American democracy, of consumer capitalism, or both?

The artifacts presented do not represent any change in form of government, but they do represent a market that is open to foreign products and consumer-driven markets.

Do they symbolize and give evidence of other things?

Answers will vary.

4. Do these photos give you insight into why people from some countries might resent American culture and, by extension, America? Why? Do they give you insight into the comments and examples made by the authors of selections included in this chapter? How?

Answers will vary.

5. Are these photographs merely documentation of reality somewhere around the globe, or do they make a stronger and more pointed argument? Can they? Does the argument they make depend on the context in which they're viewed? Why or why not?

The photos can certainly be argued to represent the soft imperialism that the United States takes part in. This case becomes stronger when the photos are seen together as a portfolio rather than mixed in with other depictions of a country.

6. Writing assignment

Classroom Exercise: focus on the world

If other countries have their own fast food, carbonated drinks, and clothing companies, why would people prefer those from the United

States? Is it attraction to the exotic? Better advertising? The appeal of modernity? Could it be that American products are the result of more research and development to make the product highly desirable, as is well documented in the case of McDonald's and Coca-Cola? Do students know of any examples abroad where a local product successfully took the market share away from an American product? This might be a good topic for the creation of political cartoons.

Diana Abu-Jaber *My Suspicious Last Name* pp. 1079–1081

1. What might Abu-Jaber mean by her closing comment, "I had no idea that being an American would ever be this hard"?

   Americans usually are able to pass freely into open foreign countries, especially when returning home. Here Abu-Jaber is being treated like an outsider.

   Why, in your opinion, might she have written this essay?

   Answers will vary.

   What might it teach you about America? About the situation of some Americans? About the situation of some who might try to come to America?

   This article presents an American system that is suspicious of foreigners and treats its own as foreigners if they resemble a racial stereotype. The reader is invited to understand what it might be like as a foreigner to face American officials and be accused of wrong doing.

2. Part of the power of Abu-Jaber's narrative of her experience results from her descriptions of the responses she received from the various immigration officers she dealt with. How would you characterize their responses to her? How might they justify their behavior if asked to do so?

   The officers sounded smug and unsympathetic to Abu-Jaber's situation. They assumed the worst until it was proven otherwise, and even then they were unapologetic. The officers might counter that they must remain unattached and professional while they proceed with the investigation and that they are often verbally abused by those that they have to hold.

What's your evaluation of the situation?

Answers will vary.

3. For Abu-Jaber, what sort of argument is one's name? What decisions has she faced and does she continue to face with respect to her name? Why?

   Abu-Jaber argues that a name is intrinsic to one's self. She has been advised to change her name, but she will not. That decision means that she will continue to be held occasionally at airports and that some people may ignore her resumé or publications because of their assumptions about what her name represents.

4. One of the tropes or kinds of figurative language that Abu-Jaber uses in this essay is one that students of rhetoric, following Aristotle, often call "the greater and the less." If you assume that Abu-Jaber is "the greater," who (or what categories of people) might be "the less," and what are you, as a reader, supposed to take from Abu-Jaber's use of this trope?

   "The less" in this case is U.S. immigration and the U.S. government in their ethnic profiling.

5. Writing assignment

Classroom Exercise: focus on the argument

Is the number of American citizens who are annually detained by immigration public information? Is there any way to learn the ethnicity of those who are detained? Is detaining anyone with a name similar to one on an official "watch list" considered racial profiling? Does it essentially serve a similar end? What alternatives can students suggest to such a system?

Yiyun Li   *Passing Through*   pp. 1082–10841

1. In what sense is Yiyun Li "passing through"?

   Li is passing through a mountain village and passing through a transitory stage of her life after which many opportunities await her.

   What argument is she making about the power of dreams? About the importance of America in the dreams of many?

   Li argues that dreaming of a better life is what led her to where she is today. She implies that one of the dreams of

many families is to have a child study in the United States and have more opportunities.

2. Why is the setting of this essay important? Why is it ironic that the events occurred in Communist China?

This story is ironic because the core of communism is an inherent equality but the author realizes that she has had an education that is unavailable to this village girl.

How have recent changes in the Chinese economy — especially the growth of capitalism there and the meteoric rise of a small but powerful, very well-to-do professional class — made the setting even more ironic?

As some rise to the professional class, others still do not have the basic needs promised by communism.

3. What was Li's initial encounter with the West? What role did her parents play in her dreams and achievements — a recurring theme among Chinese people wherever they might be around the globe?

Li first encountered a Westerner who gave her a piece of candy. Her parents encouraged her to study so that she could go to the United States.

4. What sort of ethos does Li create for herself in this essay?

Li creates for herself an ethos of empathy and introspection.

5. This selection was written by an immigrant to the United States. The previous one was written by the daughter of an immigrant. What do these stories teach us about why some people from other countries consider America a place they want to come to? Do they give you insights into why some people might not want to come to America? How do these personal narratives complement the more analytic essays in this chapter?

Immigrants come to the United States to broaden their opportunities and those of their children. From the stories, the reader can imagine the fear involved in leaving family members behind to travel to a country like America, where opportunity comes with the cost of prejudice. These personal experiences lend a different voice to the more general arguments of earlier pieces.

6. Writing assignment

Just as Li still remembers her encounter with the Westerner, it is possible that the young girl in the mountains might remember her encounter with Li as an event that caused her to ponder possibilities in her own life. Any time we are confronted with someone living a life very different than our own it raises questions about other options in the world. Have students write about a moment, big or small, in their personal experience that led them to consider a different path or propelled them along a path that they were already on.

Wrap-up Exercises for Constructing Arguments about "Why Do They Love Us? Why Do They Hate Us?"

The following assignments reflect on the chapter's theme of America's reputation in the world outside its borders. Assignment 1 is suitable for in-class essay writing.

1. Choose one of the essays that discusses the specifics of why Americans are viewed negatively abroad. Write an essay confronting the stereotypes that are presented in which you either support the portrayals or present evidence to the contrary.

2. Research a foreign newspaper in a language that you understand, and find two articles—one that is critical and one that is complementary of some recent American foreign policy or diplomatic effort. Write an essay comparing the articles with respect to the aspects of the American action that is evaluated, the generalizations that are drawn from the evaluation, the tone and ethos of the author, and your reaction to both articles.

3. Just as many Americans argue that we are misunderstood, surely misunderstandings are at the root of some stereotypes that are widely held in the United States about nations that are not our allies. Choose a nation or ethnic group with which you have some familiarity, or research a group with which you are not familiar and look at two or three stereotypes connected to that group that are widely held or acknowledged. Write an essay in which you attempt to describe, much like Medved or Hertsgaard, how these exaggerations or stereotypes may have developed and been perpetuated.